STRENGTH
OF THE
BROKEN

STRENGTH
OF THE
BROKEN

Annam M. Gordon

© 2025 by Annam M Gordon

ISBN (eBook): 978-1-968012-59-5

ISBN (softcover): 978-1-968012-60-1

ISBN (hardcover): 978-1-968012-61-8

Library Of Congress Catalog Number: 2026901066

Published in the United States of America by Lynx Publishers.

Introduction - Strength of the Broken

Most people don't think their stories matter.

They'll say, "It wasn't anything special," or, "That's just how things were."

But the truth is, some of everyday life's choices, regrets, or moments never made it into their photo album. This book is made of those broken pieces that still hit them now and then, no matter how much time has passed.

Not all dramatic. Some barely fill a paragraph. Others feel unfinished, or too ordinary to mention. And that's the point.

You'll read about heartbreak that never made a sound, love that showed up late. Anger that sat inside someone's chest so many years before it had anywhere to go. You'll meet people who held on past the breaking point, afraid of what leaving might cost them. Some stories were told to me slowly. Others spilled out like they'd been waiting years.

Every single one meant something, and I found it impossible to decide which to keep and which to hold back for later. So I put them all in, just as they came to me. Some may sound alike, but none are the same. Every story belongs to the person, and for me, every person matters. What's written here won't give you answers or clean endings. But if you're looking for something that feels true, maybe even familiar, then these stories are already yours, too, just as some of them were mine.

No Regrets, Just Growth

Regret often gets treated like something everyone has to carry. Some wish they had chosen another path, said something else, walked away sooner, or stayed longer. But I don't sit with regret like that. That doesn't mean everything turned out the way I hoped. Things fell apart, people disappointed me, and some endings came faster than I was ready for.

But those moments don't erase the fact that I made those choices because they felt right at the time. What came after taught me more than I expected. Every mistake, dead end, and goodbye forced me to see myself more clearly and face the parts of me I had been avoiding.

Real change comes from the hard parts you wish you could skip but can't. I don't see wasted time. I see lessons, proof that I lived, took risks, and learned what works for me and what doesn't. Regret keeps you stuck in the past, replaying the same scenes, wishing for a rewrite.

Growth lets you walk forward with it without staying trapped in it.

Cheaters Don't Trust Loyalty

Once someone gets caught cheating, they may apologize and promise to change, but something shifts inside them, not just for you,

but for themselves. They will never fully trust you again

because the world is now seen through their own behavior.

They get paranoid and start to think you will cheat back.

Why?

Because that is exactly what would happen if the roles were reversed. Assume everyone else operates the same way.

Guilt becomes suspicion.

Betrayal turns into constant defense. Check your phone.

Question your tone.

Accuse you of things that you are actually capable of.

A cheater is not afraid of losing you.

Just afraid of being beaten at their own game.

When someone shows you that loyalty is not in their nature, understand this: you can forgive them if you choose, but you will never receive true trust from them again.

Already broke the foundation, and deep down, know it.

Real trust cannot exist where betrayal lives.

Signs of Divided Attention

When someone puts their phone on airplane mode, turns the volume all the way down, or flips the screen over while spending time with you, it may look like a polite gesture, a way to avoid interruptions and show full focus. And sometimes, that's all it is. But often, if you look closer, there is more to it. Airplane mode is usually used for flights. So when someone uses it in your presence, it can signal that their attention isn't truly undivided. It may suggest there are people they don't want to risk being interrupted by, conversations they don't want flashing across the screen, messages they don't want you to see. Placing a phone face down works the same way. It hides the name, content, and tone of incoming notifications. On its own, it might seem harmless. But when paired with silence, airplane mode, or a locked screen, it forms a pattern. A pattern points toward the presence of other "passengers" on the flight. This doesn't automatically make someone untrustworthy, but it's often a reliable sign of divided loyalty or hidden involvement. A phone is someone's lifeline to their social world. If that connection gets shut off only when they're with you, the question is why.

What about your presence requires secrecy?

What is it they don't want to risk being seen?

The truth is simple: when someone consistently blocks all access to the outside world when they're around you, it's usually because they don't want those worlds colliding.

They're not traveling alone.

There are other passengers on that plane.

Go After the Life You Want

You don't choose a bad life. You just get used to one and fall into routines that feel safe. You wake up, do what you always do, and go to bed wondering why nothing feels exciting. You don't realize you've already made a decision. If you're not chasing what you want, you've already agreed to stay stuck. Going after the life you want isn't about motivational slogans or morning routines. Be honest and ask yourself a simple question: if your life stayed exactly the same for the next five years, would you be happy? If the answer is no, then change isn't optional. It's necessary. You wait for confidence before you act. You think once you feel ready, you'll finally start.

Confidence doesn't show up first. Action does. There's always a reason to stay in your familiar setup. You might even feel grateful for it. But being thankful for the life you have doesn't mean you have to stop wanting more. Gratitude shouldn't become a limitation. The hardest part of pursuing what you want is that nobody will hand you permission. Some people won't understand. Some may think you're being unrealistic. That's fine. It's not their job to believe in your path. It's yours. Here's what it comes down to. You can protect what's familiar and spend your days wondering what could have happened. Or you can move forward, try something new, and give yourself a shot at something better. One option feels safe. The other feels alive.

Only one takes you where you actually want to go.

The Pen Stays in My Hand

I no longer care if you make me out to be the villain in your story, as long as it keeps your dirty ink off the future pages in mine. For a long time, I fought against the way you shaped my image and twisted my intentions, believing I needed to defend myself against every whisper you allowed to spread. I wasted energy trying to correct the narrative you constructed, not realizing that the effort itself gave you more power.

Now I see that the only way forward is to leave your toxicity behind. If you want to cast me as the one who ruined what could have been, then that belongs to you. It no longer needs my participation. My life is not meant to be consumed by the twisted way you see things. You can keep that. I am finished with explanations, approval, and the weight you placed on me.

The path ahead for me will not carry your bitterness. You had your role in the earlier parts of my life, and it is already set. It cannot be erased, but it will not define the rest.

What matters is not the label you assign to me, but the chapters I have yet to write for myself.

Closure Without Satisfaction

People often speak of closure as if it were something you could request and store away. After a breakup, a loss, or the end of a project, the hope is that once the door shuts, the matter is settled. Most endings leave residue in the form of memories and questions. The difficulty lies in the gap between expectation and reality. What you need may never arrive. The shift begins when you decide to stop waiting.

This process is slow, unfolding only after revisiting the same memory once it has lost its force. When it no longer stirs new pain, its hold weakens, and you begin to move. It also does not guarantee comfort. Sometimes it leaves you resigned rather than relieved. The point is the moment when the past no longer drains your energy. In work, endings take a practical shape. Projects close when budgets expire or reports are filed. Ultimately, closure is less of a boundary than a finish line.

It is the point where you stop negotiating with what is already over. It may not feel final, but it creates enough distance to release the weight and step forward.

Real Masters of Acting Don't Live in Hollywood

You can spot real acting without ever turning on a movie. It happens in workplaces, friendships, family circles, and sometimes in people you once trusted. These aren't actors on a screen. They don't have scripts or costumes. Yet still deserving an award for performance. Truth twists like it's made of rubber. Facts bend to whatever makes them look innocent. If something goes wrong, it's never their fault. Blame shifts so smoothly you almost believe it. Hurt people and feel nothing.

No apology. No guilt. Just excuses

What makes it even more convincing is that in their own mind, they're always the hero. Rewriting the story so they appear misunderstood, clever, or even noble. Lie to save their image.

Destroying someone's peace and still sleeping fine at night.

The dangerous part is how charming this type can be.

Smiling while causing harm, speaking softly while creating chaos, acting humble, wounded, or wise.

Whatever role keeps control in their hands. You could hand out an award for Manipulation in a Leading Role, and it would be accepted proudly, unaware of the irony.

It Is What It Is

You've heard people say "it is what it is" as if that settles everything.

The phrase has no clear edges. It is not wisdom, but it carries the weight of resignation. It does not solve problems or erase difficulty.

It simply points to reality in front of you, untouched, unaltered, and unmoved by your opinion about it. When something happens to you that cannot be reversed, you only have a few options. You can fight it to the point of exhaustion, deny it until reality forces its way through, or face it. Facing it does not mean liking it. It only means acknowledging that what exists will not disappear just because you dislike it.

The phrase can feel cold when someone else says it, as if they are brushing off the weight of what matters deeply. Yet when you say it to yourself, it becomes a line that separates what can be changed from what cannot. It stops you from wasting time on fantasies of undoing what cannot be undone. You may be tempted to treat "it is what it is" as an ending. In reality, it can also be a beginning.

Once acceptance is set down, there is room for movement. If the situation is fixed, then the next step is to work with what remains. It is not about comfort. It is about clarity. The phrase carries no promise, only a mirror. For many, that mirror is enough. To see clearly what is in front of you is often the hardest part. Once you see it, even the smallest step forward becomes possible.

Your Glow Up Is Going to Hurt Some Feelings

Keeping your life to yourself? Highly recommended. A private life is basically the VIP lounge of adulthood. No freeloaders or prying questions. Just peace, snacks, and a playlist you actually like. You don't have to explain your moves or justify your choices to people who would unravel if they knew you were thriving without their approval. Like a group chat with only one member, silence is better than gossip. Now, let's talk about those people who develop a hobby called jealousy. You know the type. They're not your friends. They never were. Friends cheer you on even when you're stumbling, running on fumes. The others clap with one hand while texting with the other about how you've changed. And it isn't about growth. It's, "How dare you rise without asking our permission?" They were fine with you as long as you stayed small. The second you set boundaries and shine, you become the villain in their story. Your next chapter? It's going to sting. Picture success they didn't predict and confidence that turns heads. It'll land like a late fee they forgot about, slow and sharp. They'll remember the chances they had to show up with kindness, but they didn't. They chose distance, vanishing when you needed support. And now? They'll be watching from afar, muttering to themselves like background actors in a scene nobody asked them to perform. So go ahead. Protect your space. Live like you're the finale everyone didn't know they were waiting for. Let them face the truth that they should've been better. And if they come back with curious little questions dressed up as compliments? Smile. Hand them a spoon. Let them taste their serving of "This could've been you, if only you'd acted right."

Trust Becomes Complicated

When someone has torn apart your sense of safety, trust stops being natural. What feels automatic for others feels like walking across thin ice for you. After trauma, it feels like risk, exposing yourself to the possibility of being hurt again and giving someone power they could use to shatter you. So you pull back. You test people and hold parts of yourself back, even in relationships where you want to give more.

Walls rise because love feels dangerous when you are unsure if you can survive being broken again. You remind yourself it is protection, and maybe it is. But it also keeps you lonely even when you're surrounded by people. The world doesn't understand this hesitation. To them, you look guarded or cold. They overlook the war in your head when you think about trusting someone new. They miss the longing for connection and the ache of expecting betrayal.

The truth is, trust after trauma is not impossible. It just takes longer. It grows when proof collects slowly, when actions line up with words, and consistency begins to soften the edges of fear. That is the ground you need before you take the risk of letting someone in. And when you do, the outcomes are never the same. Sometimes they show they deserve it. Other times, they will not, and it will hurt. But either way, you're not broken for being careful. You're someone who has been through enough to understand what trust really costs.

You Learn to Live with Triggers

Triggers aren't something you choose. They show up without warning. A smell, a song, a word, a place. Suddenly, the stomach drops, the body tenses, and you're pulled back into a memory never meant to be revisited. At first, there's a fight against it. Anger for reacting, embarrassment for breaking down over something that doesn't make sense to anyone else. But over time, it becomes clear that fighting doesn't make them disappear. They're part of the terrain you have to live with. So learning begins.

What sets you off, how to breathe through it, when to leave a room, when to call someone, and how to say out loud that you are safe. Living with them is exhausting. It means always being aware, constantly scanning for danger, and planning how to handle it if something knocks you off balance. It feels unfair, and it is. But it's also proof of resilience. Strategies forming, adaptations taking root, and life continuing even with the constant threat of being pulled under. People who've never had trauma don't understand this extra layer of life.

They don't know how much energy it takes to function while managing those triggers. But you know the fight it takes every single day. And the fact that you're still here is the strongest evidence of resilience most people will never understand.

One More Dawn

It is not easy, I know. You are just lying in your bed, overthinking a million and one questions. Sleep will not come, no matter how much you wish it would. You keep creating different scenarios in your mind, imagining what you could have done, what you should have said, and if that might have changed the outcome. You trace the same circle over and over, and each time you arrive at the same conclusion. A mental list of regrets fills your thoughts, but you cannot keep blaming yourself for someone else's inability to provide the type of love you deserve. That burden does not belong to you. It is not yours to carry.

Yet the night feels endless, and you are exhausted. Everything is heavy and difficult, pressing in on you until you question whether your chest can hold it. It seems unfair that you are the one left with sleepless hours, the one who has to face the wreckage of what was supposed to be love. You find yourself asking how long it will take, how many nights will look like this. You try to bargain with yourself, to say if you can make it through one more hour, one more dawn, maybe the ache will soften. Hoping for a morning where you wake without that sting, waiting for the moment you no longer feel pulled apart by what is missing.

And even though it feels unbearable, you know the truth hidden beneath it. So take another breath. Rest your head, even if your eyes refuse to close. Let the tears fall if they need to. I promise you this storm is loud, but it will pass.

You Don't Owe Them Your Silence

There will always be those who benefit from your silence. They may not ask you outright to stay small, but their comfort rests on your decision not to speak. Silence shields their narratives, reputations, and control.

And even for you, it can feel safer to swallow words, to carry the truth in your own body so others are not disturbed by it. But unspoken words collect weight, pressing against your chest until even your breath feels borrowed.

What isn't said begins to live inside you like ghosts, haunting your memory, replaying moments of harm, convincing you that truth will never matter.

This is how everything becomes another form of violence against the possibility of healing. To speak is not always easy. Words might tremble, come out uneven, but that's not weakness. It is proof of courage. It is the sound of someone refusing to remain hidden. You don't have to be eloquent, polished, or perfect to tell the truth.

The simple act of saying what was denied or dismissed is already resistance. Silence is not owed. Not to the people who hurt you or to those who insist that peace matters more than truth. Not even to a world that warns your honesty will cause too much trouble if it is spoken aloud.

Claiming your words is how you reclaim the power that was stolen. Choosing to speak is not selfish. Often, it is an act of generosity. When one person breaks their silence, others recognize their own capacity to do the same.

Words can open locked doors for someone who thought they were the only one carrying pain. So let them be uncomfortable. Let them face what they would rather ignore.

Your voice is not a debt to be negotiated. It is a birthright, and when you decide to use it, you remind yourself and the world that you are not here to be erased. You are here to be heard.

Your story belongs to you. Speak, even when anger rises. Speak, even when bitterness lingers. Healing can look like that. Let them talk. Do not shrink or soften your truth to make it easier to dismiss.

You know what happened. You lived it. And now you speak.

Boundaries Remembered

It is natural to miss the people who once meant something to you. Memory carries both sweetness and ache, and sometimes your heart will return to the moments when their presence felt like home.

Yet missing someone does not mean you should forget why you created distance. There was a lesson in that separation, a truth about what you needed to protect within yourself. Hold both truths at once: the tenderness of missing and the strength of remembering why you walked away.

You can grieve the loss and still honor the choice that saved you. That balance lets you carry your past without being consumed by it. Healing does not erase the love you once gave, nor does it excuse the harm that forced you to step back. It simply means you refuse to trade your peace for proximity. To remember the boundary is to remember your worth, and that is how you keep yourself whole.

Not Every Goodbye Closes the Door

Goodbyes have a way of sounding final. But life doesn't always work that way. Not every one of them means forever. Just like not every ending means the story is done. Certain farewells are pauses, breaks that give you room to grow, to heal, and to see things more clearly. Sometimes stepping away is the only way to notice what you couldn't see when you were too close.

Others reveal who you are without the person you thought you couldn't live without. They strip you down, wound you deeply, but they leave you standing stronger than you ever imagined. And there are partings that circle back. People return. Not always in the same way or for the same reasons, but the thread isn't cut. Time shifts things, reshapes them, and what once broke you can come back softer.

Still, some endings are permanent. Doors really do close. And when they do, you have to honor that. It just clears space for something you never would have reached if you stayed where you were. So goodbyes aren't as final as they feel in the moment. Some open new paths. Some give you back yourself. And some teach you that endings are not the enemy. Sometimes they are the very thing that saves you.

Loyalty Isn't Real If Anyone Can Shake It

Loyalty is proven when someone tries to turn you against the people who've been good to you. If a random voice can make you question someone who's always been honest with you, that's a weakness. Solid people don't let outsiders rewrite their history. There will always be someone ready to whisper doubts, twist stories, or spread problems that don't belong to them. They act like they're protecting you, but they're only feeding drama.

Anyone who encourages you to cut off someone loyal isn't helping you. They're testing you.

If someone has shown you consistency, respect, and honesty, they've earned the benefit of the doubt. One conversation shouldn't erase years of proof. You already know who's real in your life. You don't need a second opinion.

Before you let someone poison your view, ask one question: *What's their intention?* Are they warning you because something is truly wrong or because they're jealous, bored, or out of fear of losing control? Stand on what you've seen with your own eyes. Trust your experience over someone else's commentary. Loyalty doesn't need approval from the sidelines. It just needs backbone.

I Carried You Longer Than I Should Have

There are people we hold on to long after they've let go of us. I carried you in my heart long past the moment you deserved that space. The memories, the empty promises, the way I thought it could be, as if keeping them alive would keep us alive. It weighed me down. Carrying someone who never showed for me hollowed me out.

Letting go doesn't happen in one clean moment. It comes slowly, painfully, over time. You peel your fingers back one by one from what you've been holding. You learn to stop rereading old words. You train yourself not to wait for their voice. You unclench your fists from what no longer belongs to you.

And one day, after carrying them for far too long, you wake up and realize your arms are empty. The weight is gone. It doesn't mean you never loved them or that what you felt wasn't real. It means you finally stopped breaking your own back for someone who never noticed how heavy they had become in your life.

So yeah... I carried you longer than I should have, but I don't bear your weight anymore. And that's not a loss. That's what I call freedom.

Life Without an Audience

There's something liberating about not having to share every step of your life with others. When you stop explaining yourself, the pressure eases. You no longer feel tied to outside opinions or expectations.

Life becomes yours again. In that space, the present feels fuller.

You're not rushing to frame each moment for others.

You can sit with your own thoughts, move at your own pace, and let your days unfold without needing to justify them.

The smaller details begin to stand out, and they matter in a way that isn't filtered through anyone else's view.

This isn't hiding. It's living without the constant weight of performance. The energy that once went into explaining yourself becomes energy you can use to actually live.

That is where the freedom lies: being here, in the moment, and knowing that presence itself is powerful.

Sensitivity Survives

You once believed sensitivity was a curse. You thought it made you fragile, soft, easy to break. In a world that praised toughness, you carried your tenderness as if it were shame. You told yourself that if you could harden, you would finally belong.

Sensitivity was never a weakness. It is the pulse of who you are. Remove it, and you erase conscience, empathy, intuition, and the ability to see beauty where others see nothing. It is not a flaw. It lets you feel deeply, connect to others, and turn pain into words that matter.

It is the part of you that resists numbness in a world that values coldness. Yes, sensitivity hurts. It means bleeding where others barely bruise, carrying sorrows that are not always your own, and feeling the weight of life more heavily than most.

Yet it also allows you to experience wonder more fully. A small kindness can fill you with light. The sky at dusk, the call of a bird, the trembling of a single leaf can move you to awe.

You are not weak for being sensitive. You are alive in a way many will never know.

Truth of a Broken Heart

When your heart breaks, it is not always loud. There is no clean shatter like glass against concrete. Sometimes it breaks slowly, with cracks too small to notice until one day you find yourself standing in the middle of your life and realize you can no longer hold yourself whole. The world looks the same, but something inside has collapsed. Heartbreak is not only losing someone.

It is losing the version of yourself that existed only when they were near.

Now you sit in an empty room, more present than you want to be.

Shadows cling to corners, to songs, to familiar scents, and you cannot escape them. There are nights when silence feels heavier than memory. Your chest aches as if it holds a storm it cannot release. You try to break through it, drown the emptiness with noise or movement, but nothing reaches the rawness inside.

People say time heals. Perhaps it does. Yet time does not stitch you back into who you were or return what was lost. It only teaches you to live around the absence until the weight feels like part of your body. Even with it there, you find yourself laughing at something small. For a moment, it doesn't hurt the same.

Don't Let Someone Else's Confusion Define Your Worth

Being around someone who doesn't know what they want can feel harmless at first. They're unsure, they're figuring themselves out, and you try to be patient. But if you stay too close for too long, their confusion can start to spill onto you.

When someone keeps changing their mind about you, one day warm, the next distant, it messes with your head. You start questioning yourself instead of questioning their inconsistency, wondering if you're doing something wrong. But their uncertainty has nothing to do with your value.

A person can be blind to gold and still walk past it, be handed loyalty and still hesitate, even care about you without being ready. That doesn't make you less worthy. It only makes them unprepared.

Confused people create inconsistent relationships. They drain your peace, and if you aren't careful, you'll start to lower your standards just to match their uncertainty.

That's when the real damage happens.

You stop asking, "Do they deserve me?" and start asking, "How can I convince them?"

You shift from being recognized to trying to prove you're valuable.

Your worth isn't up for debate. It doesn't change because someone else can't see it clearly. If a person doesn't know what they want, let them figure it out away from you.

Confusion is their problem. Don't let it become your identity.

Finding Who I Really Am

I have lived through what feels like a hundred versions of myself.

I tried on roles, masks, ways of being, hoping one of them would finally feel like home. None of them ever did.

I know what it means to carry sorrow. Felt the weight of memories that linger like ghosts. Spent years treating the darkness as if it were the only place I belonged.

It was familiar, even when it pressed down on me.

This time feels different.

This self does not feel like an act or a passing stage. It feels real.

For the first time, I am not hiding inside another version of myself.

I am here, as the person I was meant to be.

Every other version was preparation, fragments gathered along the way. They led me here, to a presence that finally feels whole.

The Day You Stopped Pretending

There comes a point when wearing the mask costs more than taking it off. You do not notice the weight until the smile finally snaps, stretched past its limit. The laugh rings false. The words *I'm fine* fall flat. The self-built for others gives way under its own strain. The act holds for a time. It smooths the surface, keeps others comfortable, while inside, it eats at you. Saying yes when no was needed chips away at you. Swallowed truths push your voice further down.

The mirror begins to show a stranger. The day the pretending ends is not dramatic. There is no explosion, no scene. Only a tired face that admits another day cannot be lived in a skin that does not fit. The truth doesn't shout when it first shows up. You tell it to yourself, then to others. It comes unsteady, words shaking, breaking apart as they leave you. But it is real. And real feels better than false ever did.

Not everyone stays when the cover slips. Some people walk away once the role they relied on is gone. Others grow cold when their demands are no longer met. Yet losing them is not as sharp as losing yourself once was. Keeping up the act may shield others, but it steals your peace. Ending it will not erase the pain, though it tears away the lie. That release is worth all that falls away. Life without the mask is not perfect. There are no bright surfaces to lean on. Some days open raw, certain truths weigh heavily.

But honesty holds you in a way pretense never could.

Let Them Live With Their Own Reflection

Not everyone deserves your forgiveness.

Some people knew exactly what they were doing. They caused damage and never once cared about how long it would take you to recover. They didn't make a mistake.

They made a choice. And people who deliberately cause harm shouldn't be rewarded with peace. Those people only need a mirror. They need to wake up every day next to someone just like them, someone who plays the same games, causes the same confusion, and treats them with the same carelessness they once gave you.

Only then will they understand what they put you through. Or not.

It's not revenge. It's reality.

Life has a way of circling back. Eventually, people are forced to sit in the mess they used to throw at others. You don't have to forgive them to heal. You just have to remove yourself and let life teach them what empathy never could.

You don't owe closure to someone who handed you chaos.

Oops, you Accidentally Got Better

So here's the thing. When healing begins, and the pieces start to come together, not everyone sticks around. Some disappear the moment the mess fades. It is simply what happens. Certain people were attached to the version that asked for nothing. Laughter was used to cover words that cut.

It's fine became the answer even when it was not. Convenience made it easy to keep close, the one who cleaned up the wreckage while others played the lead.

Then the words shift: Actually, no. That does not work for me.

Suddenly, it looks like horns have grown. Faces stare back as though a foreign language just slipped out. Difficult. Selfish. Changed. Correct. That is healing. Once that turn happens, the game is different. Carrying other people's chaos no longer comes first. Shrinking so someone else can stand taller is no longer on the table.

For some, that is enough reason to leave. Maybe they vanish. Maybe replies stop. Either way, the story closes with a slow fade, the realization settling that the old version is gone. Missing them is natural. Doubting the choice is natural, too. Cruelty has nothing to do with it. Honesty finally does. Anyone who only cared for the broken version was never meant for the healed one. Let them go. They already have.

Glad It's Gone

People love saying, "You never know what you have until it's gone," like it's some deep life lesson.

They say it with that wise face, waiting for you to nod along. Well, I knew exactly what I had.

And I was counting the minutes until it left.

Not everything that disappears deserves a memorial. Some things belong in the recycling bin. Some people walk out of your life, and the air gets cleaner. Everyone expects sadness when things end. They wait for the dramatic breakdown. Sorry to disappoint.

Sometimes the real reaction is relief.
Not crying on the floor. More like shrugging and saying,

"About time."

Let them call it harsh. Let them say you should be more sentimental. Fine. They can miss it.

I will not because losing something toxic is not a loss. It is pest control.

So yes, I knew what I had.

And believe me, I am thrilled it is gone.

Cowardice Was Your Legacy

I've grown so much since I left you. Strength has taken root where I once felt small. Kindness finally extends to myself in ways it never did before. Still, sometimes,

I catch myself wondering if you would even recognize me now.

Would this version of me change the way you looked at me?

Or alter the way you acted?

The questions linger, but the answers do not matter.

What does matter is the memory that when I needed you most, you were nowhere to be found. That truth remains the same. Your cowardice.

In contrast, the person I am now has no place for you.

Those Who Pretend

Don't waste your energy on those who rage in the open. With them, the fight stands in front of you, and you know exactly what you face.

The harder wound comes from the ones beside you who pretend to care. They wear kindness like a mask and wait until your guard is low.

What looks like comfort is simply preparation for the blow. It arrives when you are stretched thin. One moment unsettles you, and you cannot name why. Another leaves you doubting yourself. By the time the truth is clear, trust has already slipped away.

Yet betrayal does not finish you. To see it is to strip away its disguise.

To name it is to take back your ground. What is solid in you does not fade when others fall short. Growth continues, with or without them. Nothing they twist can take that away.

Where I Could Breathe

They asked me why I didn't want to be around those people anymore. The truth wasn't one big reason. It was a hundred small moments I wished I could unsee. The way they talked about each other when someone wasn't around, the tone, the smirks, the small cuts disguised as harmless jokes. Then they sat at the same table. Laughed as if nothing cruel was said. Smiled for pictures. Said "I love you" while rolling their eyes, the second someone turned away. I couldn't sit in that and share food with people who poisoned the air behind your back and called it friendship to your face.

What I felt wasn't anger.

It was heavier, something closer to grief, like losing people who were still alive. Because the version I cared for was gone, if it was ever real at all. Around them, I felt smaller, guarded, as if parts of me had to stay hidden or else be passed around for laughs later. Affection in that space was conditional. Loyalty was spoken, not lived. So now, this wasn't drama, fight, or bitterness. It was me finally seeing that sitting at that table cost too much of my peace, and I would rather eat where I could breathe.

Not Another Copy

The world does not need another copy.

It needs your voice as it really is, shaped by what you've lived and how you see things. Imitation is easy, but it erases the parts of you that matter most.

When you hide behind what sounds safe or familiar, you trade honesty for comfort, and the truth you carry never makes it out. Your perspective is not supposed to match anyone else's. It is meant to stand out on its own, even if it feels rough or small.

What makes your voice worth hearing is not that it sounds polished or popular but that it comes from you. No one else has your history, your scars, or the way you put words together. If you do not speak in that voice, the world loses something it will never get from anywhere else.

Crossing Into Something New

Most people eventually pause and think about what comes next.

Picture yourself standing in front of a doorway. You know that if you walk through it, life will shift in some way. Before taking that step, you look back at what brought you here. Everyone carries memories. Some feel warm. Others sting or feel unfinished. There are choices you wish had gone differently and people you wish you could hold one more time. There are also personal victories you forget to give yourself credit for.

The hard part isn't deciding whether to move forward. Life moves either way. The real choice is what you take with you. Some things deserve a place in your hands. Lessons from past mistakes. Relationships that support you. Values you stand by no matter what. Other things don't earn that right. Old guilt that solves nothing. Anger that loops the same story in your head. Constant comparison. Worry about what others think. These don't lead you anywhere useful. They cling to you and make each step heavier. Moving forward doesn't require perfection. It requires honesty.

You can say, "I did what I could with what I knew. I know more now. I'm ready to act like it." A new beginning isn't a miracle. It's a decision. Keep what builds you. Leave what drains you. Then walk through the doorway.

Delusion in Disguise

The most dangerous people are the ones who believe they are good. They twist every story until they look like the hero, shift every outcome until they escape fault, and walk away without owning anything. In their minds, they have never caused harm, yet everyone around them ends up carrying the damage. Nothing is ever their fault; every flaw is redirected, and every problem pushed onto someone else.

That blindness makes them harder to face than someone openly cruel, because you cannot argue with a person who has already convinced themselves they are righteous. You can show them proof, name the harm, lay out the facts, but they will not see it. That refusal makes them dangerous, not only to others but to themselves, because it allows them to keep moving through life untouched by accountability.

What they carry is not goodness but delusion, and when delusion is paired with confidence, it can wreck everything it touches.

Mistakes Are Often the Beginning of Masterpieces

Mistakes are not the end of the story. They mark the place where real work starts. Failure shows you what will not hold and forces you to find another way. A masterpiece grows out of that. What looks solid in the end is built on broken attempts beneath it. Struggle is not a decoration around the work. It is the frame that holds it up. The value of failure is that it teaches what success never could. It builds toughness, demands patience, and proves how far you are willing to keep going. Nothing lasting comes clean. The path is uneven, filled with trial and error, and each wrong move is part of what makes the final piece stand.

False Mask of Strength

Rudeness isn't strength. It's the shortcut people take when they don't have the patience or the courage to show real power. Anyone can snap, insult, or talk over someone. That doesn't take grit. Real strength is control, holding yourself back when you could crush someone. Rudeness is cheap and loud, but it's hollow. It comes from people who feel small and want to look bigger. They confuse fear with respect and noise with authority. You don't need to tear someone down to prove you can stand tall. That's what the weak do when they can't figure out how to carry themselves.

Strength shows in how you handle pressure when eyes are on you, the way you deal with people who can't give you anything back, and when you take a hit and keep moving without lowering yourself. That kind of power doesn't need a spotlight or a stage. It speaks for itself, and it doesn't let you fold when the easiest choice is to snap. That's where the difference is drawn, between the ones who pretend to have power and the ones who truly hold it.

His Endless Hunger

A lustful man will never find his limit in one woman.

A good woman can be at home, and still his eyes keep roaming. It doesn't matter how deeply you give yourself, he will keep reaching for what isn't his. Flirting, texting others behind your back, looking for attention like it's air. No amount of beauty, devotion, or fire will fill the black pit in him. You can change your hair, your body, even your whole life around him, and it still won't matter. There is always the thought that something else is out there. He will compare, even when there's nothing to compare.

A man ruled by desire does not see loyalty as enough, only what has not yet been taken. The chase matters more than the woman already standing with him. His thirst is endless, and nothing you offer can satisfy it. You'll run yourself down trying to keep up, while he searches for the next woman to notice him. The sad truth is, he can't survive without being noticed by other women. Take away that attention, and what's left is a shell of a man, hollow and weak.

Walking on Thin Ice

I kept expecting you to change, and the whole time it ended up being me. Didn't even notice at first. Talking less and less. Walking into a room started to feel heavier than it should. It got easier to nod along instead of saying what was really on my mind.

Laughed at things even when they weren't funny, and the stuff that hurt just got shoved down and never brought up. After a while, all the anger turned into silence. Started calling that patience, like being the bigger person, but honestly, it was just being stuck.

Kept saying it was love, like that explained why shrinking made sense. Thought it was a strength, yet it was only pretending. Insisted it was maturity, but it was just giving up.

By the end, I had erased myself to keep the peace.

And once that was clear, it couldn't be unseen. The peace I held onto wasn't even real. Every day felt like walking on thin ice, careful steps, waiting for cracks.

The more careful my steps became, the less of me there was left.

When Change Is Just a Costume

Certain people say they have changed, yet nothing underneath is different. Growth never happens, only better disguises. One excuse gets traded for another. Old lies get polished into cleaner versions. The words sound wiser and more refined, but the meaning stays empty. From afar, it can look like a transformation. Social media posts about healing and reinvention. Claims of new priorities. Speeches about accountability. It all reads well until something real is placed in their hands. Trust is offered, the pattern repeats. Disappointment is only the surface cut. The deeper wound settles in the person who believed. Trust turns into doubt. Doubt into self-blame. Quiet questions begin to echo.

Why didn't I see it sooner? Was I foolish? Did I expect too much?

But misplaced trust is not a flaw, just as hope is not a weakness. Some people never planned to change. Only planned to be seen differently. Real change does not perform online. It does not lean on pretty words. It proves itself slowly through action that holds steady. Costumes may fool the eye. Repeated patterns do not. Eventually, it becomes clear. Instead of watching the show, it is better to walk out of the theater.

Another Happiness

Brokenness changes the way you move through the world. It takes away what you thought you could never lose, and when that space opens up, your eyes start catching things you never slowed down enough to see. The morning air doesn't just pass you anymore; you feel it on your skin, reminding you that you are still alive. A hand on your shoulder doesn't feel casual; it feels like proof you're not walking through this alone.

Even the sunlight pouring across the same floor you've crossed for years doesn't look like the same thing. It lands different, feels like a gift, one you might not have noticed if life had stayed untouched. These small things rise up once the bigger pieces fall apart. They don't erase the pain or cover what broke, but they do make the ground beneath you stronger than you thought it could be. They tell you there is still something worth leaning on. You start to understand that what you thought was ordinary carries a strength you had overlooked. The smile of a stranger, the way a tree bends but does not break in the wind, these details carry you.

And without planning it, you find yourself gathering these pieces. They don't add up to what you had before, but they form something different. You stop chasing the picture of how you thought life should look and begin to live inside what is actually here. The brokenness doesn't disappear, and the cracks don't close, but you learn to let the light come through them. This is where another form of happiness grows. Not the one you once imagined. It is different, and it grows out of what remains.

Progress Brings New Sadness

Many people assume that once they start to heal, they will only feel happier and lighter. The reality is more complicated. As progress is made, a different sadness can show up. And that is not a failure or a step backward. It happens when the mind is finally strong enough to recognize losses that were too overwhelming to face before. At first, healing feels like relief. The pressure that held you down finally loosens. You notice small moments of peace returning, and you may even catch yourself laughing again. Yet with each step forward, new layers rise. Healing does not erase what happened. It simply gives you the strength to look at the parts you once turned away from. And when those parts surface, they bring grief with them. It is not a weakness. It is the mind and heart working together to face what was left unfinished.

As you grow, you discover that grief and healing are not opposites. They walk side by side. One reminds you of the loss, the other keeps teaching you that loss does not end your life. This mixture is what gives healing its depth. Moving forward does not mean forgetting. And carrying pain for a while does not cancel joy. With time, this ache settles into something you can live with. It softens, changes shape, and becomes part of the story without controlling it. And as you continue, you realize progress is not about escaping that feeling. It is more about learning how to keep going with it without shutting you down. Healing is not only lightness. It is the courage to face both the ache and the hope, and to let them exist together.

How We Rebuild

Life does not ask permission before it knocks us down. One day, we think we know where things are headed, and the next, everything feels cracked open. In those moments, nothing feels polished or neat. We wake up heavy, sit with the ache, and wonder if the ground will hold. That is where growth begins. Not in rushing to cover the hurt, but in letting ourselves feel it fully. It's in the slow act of learning how to live inside the mess without losing hope. It is the decision to stand back up, even when standing feels harder than falling. It is looking at the pieces scattered around us and saying: I will not waste what broke me, I will shape it into something new. This is everyday strength. It is not about quick recovery or flawless courage. It is about showing up and carrying forward the wisdom carved into us by struggle. What breaks us does not define us. How we rebuild does.

When Something Real Begins

When something real begins, it doesn't feel like it just enters your life; it rewrites it. You start to notice that the old stories don't hold you the way they once did. The pain, the disappointments, even the pieces you thought you'd never let go of, stop defining you. They belong to a version of yourself that no longer walks into the room with you.

A new love carries a feeling you didn't know existed. It offers what the past never gave. And what surprises you most is how natural it feels. The past loses its pull. You stop reaching for what used to hurt. Trust comes easier than you expected, and you begin to believe it was always meant for you.

Tired, but I Have Goals

There are days when everything presses so hard against you that even opening your eyes feels like work. Fatigue settles into the body, the mind, and every step taken. Tired becomes the language of survival. Yet beneath that heaviness, a pulse refuses to go silent. A voice speaks from somewhere deeper: I have goals. Those four words shift the horizon. They mean defeat has not won, and the soul has not surrendered. To say those words when you are close to giving up is defiance in the face of exhaustion. It is a vow that even though rest feels overdue and strength feels distant, something worth chasing still lives inside you.

They are the compass when energy runs low. They are proof that your story has direction, even if the pages turn slowly. Weariness may slow the stride, but it cannot erase the destination. It may blur the vision, but it does not blind the purpose. Every step, no matter how small, is progress. Holding on to what matters is proof of endurance. It shows that even in struggle, you are still carrying a dream. And that changes everything.

I Got Out on My Own

For a long time, I lived through things I did not know how to talk about. I stayed silent because speaking felt dangerous. Every time I tried to stand up for myself, it only got worse. So I learned to make myself small. I shut down just to survive.

There was constant fear. Real physical fear. I was hit, threatened, and humiliated. I was not seen as a person, more like something to control. I was hurt in ways that still live in my body. Some days, I cannot even walk. Some nights, I did not think I would wake up in the morning.

What made it even harder was knowing it came from someone I trusted. Someone who claimed to love me.

One day, I finally understood that staying would kill me, either slowly or suddenly. No one was coming to help me. So I left. I was scared and shaking and unsure of what would come next, but I left. That was the moment everything changed.

People think healing means forgiving or forgetting. It does not. I remember everything, and I probably always will. The difference is that those memories do not control me anymore. They do not own my future.

Today I live differently. I have peace. I have safety. I have people in my life who do not make me flinch when they move. I laugh without pretending. I rest without fear. I saved myself.

I have many scars, both visible and invisible, but they remind me of one thing. I got out. I survived.

No one will ever take my freedom again.

Survival on Autopilot

When you reach the point where you whisper to yourself, *all the joy has been taken away from me. I'm not living, just existing.* It feels like standing in a world where the colors have drained out, and you're moving through life as if it's happening to someone else. It feels like survival on autopilot. That truth is heavy. No need to dress it up.

But here is what's real. Even in that space, the part of you that notices the emptiness is the same part that is still searching for life. The fact that you can name it means you still have something in you that refuses to die out. That spark is small, but it's stubborn. It will wait for you. Living again does not happen all at once. It always sneaks back in a laugh you did not expect, in the way the sky looks when the sun sets just right, in a song that makes you feel alive. Slowly, what was flat begins to take shape again.

You may not feel joy right now, but you are not sentenced to numbness forever.

One Second Can Feel Like a Lifetime

We often treat one second like nothing. Too small to matter. Gone before it even lands. That changes when someone is waiting for something important. When a person is hoping for news and finds themselves trapped between yes and no. Between loss and relief. Between life as it was and life as it might become. In that kind of moment, one second stretches. Ask someone who has waited for a phone call from a doctor. A message from someone they love. A reply that could save or end a relationship. They will say one second is not quick. It becomes heavy. Thoughts rush in. Every outcome rises and falls in the mind. Hope flickers while doubt grows louder. Seconds feel like entire hours. Waiting turns into a test of belief. You begin confidently. Certain that everything will be fine. You repeat reminders to stay calm. To think clearly. Yet as time drags, your trust in the outcome wears thin. The silence around you becomes stronger than spoken words. Your mind whispers that maybe the answer you fear is already real. This kind of waiting teaches something simple. Time is not ruled by clocks. It is ruled by emotion. Joy moves fast. Painful pauses slow everything down. Those who wait understand this better than anyone. So when someone says they are waiting, do not dismiss them. Do not tell them to relax or distract themselves. Waiting is not easy. It is a fight between holding on and letting go. One second can feel endless when hope begins to fade. Yet sometimes that same second is the one where everything shifts. That is why people keep holding on, even when it hurts. Because letting go too early might mean missing the moment things finally turn in their favor.

Those Who Have Walked Through Darkness Understand Light

People who have been broken often end up loving with a strength that feels uncommon. They do not take affection for granted. That memory of emptiness stays inside them, and it changes the way they give.

When someone has lived in the dark, even the smallest act of kindness becomes something they can treasure. A smile, a gentle word, the presence of someone who stays. These things are noticed with a tenderness that comes only from having once lived without them.

This is why their love is unmatchable. They have learned, sometimes painfully, that the warmth from another soul is not guaranteed. And when they do find it, they hold it with both hands, treating it as if it were the rarest thing on earth.

The Body Keeps the Score Even When You Don't Want It To

You can tell yourself the past is behind you. The mind can be convinced that it is safe now, but your body doesn't always believe it. It keeps the memory even when release is all you want. Flashbacks. Nightmares. Sudden fear in a calm room. A racing heart when someone raises their voice. Muscles tightening at footsteps behind you. The memory stays. This is one of the cruelest parts of trauma. It doesn't live only in thought. It roots itself in the nervous system. The whole self can flinch, freeze, react as if danger is happening again, even when it isn't.

Then comes the anger. The names you call yourself. The question of why relaxation seems impossible. But it isn't a weakness. It is biology. It is the way your body tried to protect you, not knowing the danger had ended. People on the outside don't see it. To them, it looks like moodiness or paranoia.

What they call overreaction is actually survival instinct on repeat. Even when explained, most will never understand what it's like to live inside a body that refuses to forget. Healing isn't just about thinking differently. It's about retraining the body to believe the present is safe. That takes time and patience. Until then, life carries the weight of a body that remembers too much.

It's not your fault. It never was.

It's Not the Same Kind of Happy

She's happy. She wakes up next to him every morning and still can't quite believe it. The way he smiles at her before he's even fully awake. The warmth of his hand under the covers when he pulls her close. This is what she wanted: to be with him, to start a new life together. And she has it now. But still, some days feel heavy. It's not that anything's wrong. It's just... Everything is different. Even though the streets are familiar, so many things feel like a puzzle. She doesn't always know the right words to say, not in the way that feels natural, easy. Back home, everything made sense. Here, even the small things, ordering a sandwich, come with this subtle friction. She misses things she never expected to miss. The way the sky looked from her old bedroom window. Her favorite café, where they constantly remembered her order. The rhythm of her language rolls off her tongue without second-guessing. And she's tired. Starting over takes energy. New routines, new people. His family tries, filling her plate, learning her favorite things, making room for her laughter at their table. She feels their honest, unfiltered love toward her, even when her heart is homesick. It's exciting, yes, but exhausting too. He holds her through it. Listens when she cries for reasons she can't explain. He doesn't try to fix it; just reminds her they're building something together. And she believes him. It's just not the same kind of happy she knew before.

And maybe that's the whole point. It doesn't have to be.

I Can't Keep Starting Over With You

I do not trust you. I wanted to trust you. I tried to. Every time I let my guard down and let you closer, I hoped things would finally be different. But it keeps happening the same way. I start to believe you mean well, I begin to relax, and then you do something that knocks everything back to the beginning. One step forward, ten steps back. Again and again. After a while, it stops feeling like progress and starts feeling like a trap. Trust is not built on big promises. It comes from feeling safe. I should not have to question your intentions every time your tone shifts or wonder who I am dealing with from one day to the next. I am tired of rebuilding the same bridge only for you to burn it the moment I step on it. Tired of waiting for the next disappointment. I cannot keep living in this cycle of hoping and getting hurt. It is not healthy. It is not fair. It is not love. So no, I do not trust you. I want a connection that moves forward, not one that keeps dragging me back to square one. I do not hate you. I just refuse to relive the same pain over and over. If trust cannot grow here, then I have to grow past this.

Actions Prove What Words Can't

People often describe themselves with confidence. They say they're loyal, kind, or reliable. That's useful to hear, but it's not enough. Words only show how someone *wants* to be seen. To understand how someone thinks, listen to how they talk about others if every conversation turns into gossip or blame, that reveals their mindset. If they speak with fairness, that's a sign of maturity. Speech shows mental habits.

But when it comes to trust, actions are the only proof. Someone who claims to care and promises effort but never follows through is not committed. They only like sounding supportive.

It's simple: words are a preview; actions are the reality.

Instead of getting impressed by what people *say*, check how they behave when it costs them time, comfort, or advantage. That's when real character shows.

Listen to words. Judge by actions. Only trust when both lines up.

What Helps You Heal

That's a powerful question, and it doesn't have a simple answer, especially when pain and history are involved. Whether to hate or love someone often depends on what they did to you and what they did for you, and how those things live inside you now. Some people do both. They harm us and help us. They give us something meaningful and also leave us bleeding. You don't have to pick just one feeling. Love can be in one hand and anger in the other. Mourning what was given can live alongside fury for what was taken. That's human.

But hate is heavy. It burns through the person holding it, not the one who caused it. Sometimes it feels necessary, like a shield or a protest, but over time it reshapes you into someone unfamiliar. That doesn't mean forgiving or forgetting. It means deciding how much space they get inside you, and whether their actions shape your heart or only your history. And love? Love can be dangerous if it keeps pulling you back into harm. But it doesn't always mean trust or reunion. Sometimes it's only the memory of what was good, carried without letting it erase what was cruel. So maybe the question isn't hate or love. Maybe it's this: What helps you heal? What helps you return to yourself? Let that be the compass.

Guilt Runs

When someone knows they've treated you poorly, their absence often speaks louder than any apology ever could. Guilt has a way of chasing them out of the room, leaving silence where accountability should have stood. It's easier for them to vanish than to face the truth of their own behavior. Apology demands courage. Respect requires maturity.

But some people would rather rewrite the story in their own minds than admit they were wrong in yours. So they remove themselves, not as an act of mercy, but as proof of the conscience they can't quiet.

Their avoidance isn't your loss. It's their confession.

That Loss Is Yours

And you're shocked? No woman will ever hand you what she did: patience, forgiveness, and the belief that you could grow.

She never wanted to control who you were; she only wanted the harm to end. But your pride and your need to play the victim chained you to the same toxic cycle, leaving her trapped in promises you never kept.

She gave you something rare, trust that most will never offer twice.

That faith is gone. And the loss is yours alone.

No One Came

You were never protected. Nobody stepped in when harm came your way. That absence forced you to grow faster than you should have. You had to make choices, carry burdens without support, and face consequences alone. Over time, you stopped expecting anyone to intervene. Independence wasn't chosen; it was pressed onto you until it became second nature. What should have broken you carved resilience into your bones.

No one saved you. You carried yourself through.

Twisted Ties

Sometimes we hurt those who need us, and need those who hurt us. That's the loop we get caught in. The people who show up for us fade into the background, overlooked and taken for granted.

Their care doesn't light the same fire in us, because it doesn't echo the chaos we've learned to call love. Instead, we chase the ones who keep us uncertain. We bend for their attention, bleed for their approval, and stay hooked on the sharp edge of their absence.

We call it passion, but it's only the familiar sting of absence.

If I Was Worth So Little to You, Why Did You Stay?

Tell me what I did to make you treat me so cheaply.

I keep going over everything in my head, trying to find the moment I lost value in your eyes. Was it when I forgave you too easily? When did I stay after the first red flag? When I believed your excuses instead of trusting my own instincts? I keep wondering if I taught you how to treat me. Maybe I made it too easy for you to take without giving anything back, and you got used to my patience and mistook it for weakness.

Maybe you knew I would always come back, so you stopped trying. What hurts the most is that I did not ask for much. I only wanted respect. Honesty. Effort. Basic human decency. Yet somehow, even that felt like too much for you to offer consistently.

So now I am left asking myself a different question. Why did I let you? I see it clearly now. I stayed longer than I should have. I accepted crumbs and called it love. But I do not want your answer or your explanation. I already understand. You treated me cheaply because you never learned how to value anything real. And I allowed it because I was still learning how to value myself. That part is over now. I will not ask you again why you did what you did.

The only question that matters now belongs to me, and I already know the answer. I deserved more. And you deserve to stay exactly where you are without me.

Unspoken Battles

There are people walking through hard days, carrying a darkness they don't share. They stay silent since speaking up feels dangerous. They know the moment they open their mouth, it won't bring comfort. It'll bring whispers. Instead of being lifted, they'll be picked apart, and their pain turned into talk for others to pass around. So they hold it in. They aren't fine, but the world has shown them that honesty is treated like weakness, and struggle becomes entertainment.

And in that silence, the burden grows, while the chance of being understood slips further away.

Silent Defiance

They're angry because nothing they put in your path broke you. Every barrier they raised, you found a way past without hesitation. What cuts deeper is that you never spoke about it. You didn't draw attention to it or ask for recognition; you just kept moving forward.

Your silence stings more than any response, because it shows them the truth: they lost the power they thought they had over you, and every ounce of energy they spent trying to stop you was wasted.

The Word Inside You

The word inside you is too big to stay in the corner. It was never meant to be contained. It presses against the walls you have built, waiting for the moment you trust it enough to step out into the open. A word like that carries more than sound. It holds your history, your ache, your courage, and all that you have kept in silence. When you finally let it rise, it does not emerge fragile. It is certain and alive. You were never meant to stay small. Speaking, naming, and bringing forward the truth you have been holding has always been yours to claim. The world may not be ready, but the beginning rarely asks permission. It just arrives and changes everything.

And so are you.

Their Shield

There are people who hurt you and then act like it never happened. They brush past the damage, as if your pain doesn't matter. Then, when they need a story, they twist the truth and speak against you, playing the victim in their own tale. This is their shield. It is the only defense they know. They raise it high to block the truth, hide behind it to win sympathy, and depend on it because, without it, everything they have done is exposed. To drop it would mean facing the truth, and the truth is the one thing they fear most.

Grieving as a Core Part of Healing

Healing is not only about feeling better in the present. It also asks us to grieve the past. That grief can take many forms: sadness for years that slipped away, anger at those who failed us, or sorrow for the versions of ourselves who carried burdens they never should have borne. Some grieve the childhood they never got to enjoy. Others mourn the chances lost in the shadow of illness. This process is not optional. It is part of recovery itself, helping us face what was real and still choose to move forward instead of giving up.

Pain Creates Kindness

Kindness is rarely born from comfort. The people who step up first or lift others the most are often the ones who have carried the deepest pain. Someone who knows real loneliness understands how painful it is to feel left out. Because of that, they pay extra attention when someone seems withdrawn. They do not want anyone else to go through that same feeling, so they reach out first, remembering what it felt like when no one reached out to them. The same happens with people who seem upbeat all the time. You might think they smile because their life is great. In reality, they have probably learned to smile so others won't worry. They know what it is like to feel hopeless, so they go out of their way to keep others from feeling the same. Their humor is not always joy; sometimes it is a shield.

People who have been hurt repeatedly often learn early how fast life can change. They stop judging quickly, listen more, and notice details others miss. Their understanding is not from reading books. It comes from living through situations that forced them to study how people behave when they are in pain.

None of this means suffering is a good thing. It should not be romanticized. But some turn their experience into empathy.

The world would be better if more people understood that kindness is not always a sign of ease. Sometimes it is survival. The friend who checks in on you might be the one who was never checked on. The one who makes you laugh might still cry in private. Instead of assuming someone is fine because they act strong, we should remember that the strongest behavior often comes from the deepest pain.

Recognizing Missed Experiences

When healing begins, we often notice how much of life we were kept on the sidelines of. Someone who lived for years in depression might look back at the milestones that slipped by, school events, friendships, or early career steps that never had space to grow. A person raised in a stressful or unsafe home might see how much of their joy and freedom was lost along the way.

And sometimes the losses come through relationships. When you spend years tied to someone who drains you or keeps you walking on edge, you begin to see how much happiness never had room to take root. The laughter that could have filled those days, the ease that might have been there, the simple chance to feel at peace, all of it was crowded out. These realizations bring sadness, because they show us not only what we lived through, but also what we never got to live at all.

Silence Speaks Louder Than I Do

Not every truth needs to be shouted, and not every wound needs words. I've learned that people hear what they want when I speak. They twist words until what was raw becomes unrecognizable. Silence leaves them alone with themselves. It makes them sit with what they've done. They think my silence means I'm blind, too naive to notice, but it is not the same as ignorance. I could answer them. I could throw their words back and let anger do the talking. I could set every bridge on fire just to prove a point. And maybe for a moment, it would feel good. But I know myself too well to waste my energy that way. There's a strength in refusing to answer. When someone tries to bait you into cruelty, restraint becomes a barrier they can't cross. They push, dig, demand, and you give them nothing. That nothing hits harder than any comeback. It is not only about conflict. Sometimes it is grief, the sort of pain that doesn't fit inside words. I've stood in rooms where I could have explained my hurt, but the heaviness in my chest made language too small. In those moments, silence became my only honest expression. Tears fell, my body shook, but my lips stayed closed. Words would have made the truth smaller, not clearer. It can also be love. Sitting beside someone who understands without asking. The wordless bond that holds you firm, that feels like safety instead of emptiness. That presence speaks more than all the "I love yous" in the world. People underestimate the unsaid. They think it means weakness or that you don't know what to say. But the absence of words is layered. It can be protection, defiance, grief, or the deepest intimacy. I don't waste my words anymore. I let them be sharp when needed, soft when I choose, but never thrown carelessly. And when language won't serve me, I let silence do the talking. Sometimes the unsaid is the loudest truth of all.

Don't Let Your Word Leak Away

Your word is all you really have. Not the promises made when life feels light, but the ones spoken when you're tired, when showing up costs you something. That's where trust is proven. That's where people learn who you are. It doesn't take much for your word to slip. You might say yes while knowing the answer is no, or agree to something you never intend to finish. At first, it feels small, easy to excuse, but people remember. And deeper still, you remember. Each time you go against your own word, you cut into yourself. Integrity is not a grand gesture. It isn't about speeches or being known as a good person. It shows up in the small choices: returning the call when you said you would, paying back what you owe, keeping the promise you made to your partner, admitting when you're wrong instead of letting silence bury it.

Those moments build you up or strip you down. No one holds their word perfectly. We all fall short. But when it slips too often, trust is broken. And once that trust is gone, it takes years to rebuild, if it can at all. The truth is, your word isn't first for other people. It's for you. When you keep it, you learn you can trust yourself. And once you trust yourself, you move differently in the world. You walk into rooms standing tall, no longer waiting for someone else to hand you worth. So guard your word. Spend it with care. Offer it only where you're willing to stand behind it. And when you speak, let it matter. Let it cost something.

Your word is the backbone of who you are. Without it, everything else falls apart.

Nights You Don't Admit Out Loud

There are nights after heartbreak that you don't tell anyone about. Nights when the room feels too big, and you drink too much, staring at the ceiling for hours, waiting for sleep that never comes. So you grab your phone, scroll through old pictures until your vision blurs, delete them all, then dig them out of the trash again. These times don't look romantic or dramatic. They look like you sitting on the floor, surrounded by clothes you don't remember pulling out of the closet. You're trying so hard not to call, giving in anyway, then hanging up before the line connects.

Other times, you don't eat for two days, then suddenly eat until you feel sick. Nobody warns you that heartbreak makes you act strange. It rewires your brain, leaves you forgetting things, and repeating questions until you barely recognize your own voice. These hours aren't the ones you post about. They're the ones you survive in silence, hating yourself for how small you feel. But they are real. And they change you in ways the good days never could. It strips away every illusion of strength and control, leaving you raw in the worst way. Survival isn't always standing tall. Sometimes it's crawling across the carpet at three in the morning, clutching your chest, hoping the ache loosens for just a second.

Running From the Past

You think you can run from the past. Box it up in your mind and shove it to the back. Promise yourself you will never return. So you start over. Move to a new place, meet strangers who do not know your story, fill your days with new habits that make it feel like the old ones never happened. Tell yourself that if the door is slammed hard enough, everything will stay sealed away. But the past does not stay sealed. It barges back in and interrupts the life you are trying to build. It can take over a simple afternoon, turn a face in the crowd into a reminder, pull you out of the present before you even know what happened.

And in those moments, you see that running never erased it. It only delayed the meeting.

The Worst Part About Being Lied To

The worst part about being lied to isn't the lie itself. It's realizing you'll never know which parts of the past were real. One lie forces you to question everything else that person said or did. Every conversation turns suspicious. Every memory feels edited. You start doubting your own judgment. You trusted someone who hid the truth from you. Now you don't know if you misread them or if they were just good at pretending. A lie doesn't only break trust. It breaks clarity. You're left with guesses instead of answers. And the person who lied still knows which parts were fake while you're stuck sorting through the mess. That's what makes lying so damaging. It doesn't just change in one moment.

It rewrites all the ones before it.

Ghosts Don't Always Haunt Houses

Ghosts don't always haunt houses. Sometimes they rise in the middle of your day: a song that stops you cold, a trace of perfume drifting past, a street that pulls you back to what you lost. They aren't trapped in walls or basements. They travel with you, showing up when you least expect them. These ghosts don't rattle chains. Memory carries them back, slipping into the places you thought were safe. The past isn't gone just because you walked away. And the hardest truth is that you can't move out of yourself. Wherever life takes you, they follow. You can't evict them. You just learn to live with the fact that some rooms inside you will always be occupied by someone who isn't coming back.

Apology That Never Came

You tell yourself you don't need it. That closure is a myth; that you can move forward without hearing the words. But deep down, you wait for it. That apology. That acknowledgment that you weren't crazy, that your pain wasn't imagined. It never comes. Days turn into months, months into years, and nothing. Yet you still wait for them to admit it. To say they were wrong. Instead, you get silence. And that feels like a second betrayal. Like the wound wasn't enough, they had to salt it by pretending it never happened.

So you're left with unfinished sentences in your chest. But after a time, you realize something harder: even if they said it, it wouldn't erase what happened. It wouldn't change who they showed themselves to be. You were waiting for words to clean up what actions had already destroyed. And words can't do that.

You're Not Lazy

You're not lazy, just exhausted from fighting battles nobody knows about. Battles you never speak of, because it feels easier to stay silent than explain. Every day, you push yourself through routines that feel heavier than they should. People don't see that truth. They notice undone tasks, blank stares, and the lack of energy, and they assume you don't care. What they miss is the effort it takes just to hold yourself together. The sleepless nights when your head won't shut off. The mornings when you drag yesterday into today. Fighting in silence takes more from you than most people will ever understand. It drains you until even the smallest things feel impossible. So stop calling yourself lazy.

That word doesn't belong to you. You are not unmotivated, just completely drained at this time, and that's a big difference.

Bad Treatment Can Feel Familiar

If you don't feel good about yourself, you can end up spending time with people who treat you badly.

Why?

Because part of you already believes you don't deserve better.

When someone is kind to you, it can feel uncomfortable. Compliments don't land. Support feels strange. You start wondering if they're lying or if they just don't know the "real" you yet. Good treatment feels like a mistake. Bad treatment feels familiar. So you settle. You put up with rude comments, cold behavior, or being ignored. It feels bad, but in your mind, it matches the opinion you already have of yourself. It confirms the story in your head: I'm not that important. I shouldn't expect much. This is what I get. The sad part is that you might defend people who hurt you while doubting the ones who try to care. You push away the good and accept the bad. But how others treat you often reflects how you treat yourself on the inside. If you believe you're worthless, you stop asking for respect. If you believe you matter, you stop tolerating disrespect. The real work isn't just walking away from toxic people. It's changing what you believe about yourself, so kindness doesn't feel suspicious and basic decency feels normal, not like a gift you have to earn.

Betrayal Ends Friendship

You cannot call someone a friend if they were the one who broke your trust and left your heart in pieces. The people who drained you of hope and energy don't get to walk with you into the future. They already showed you what they do with the place you gave them. A true friend doesn't treat the love or loyalty you offered carelessly.

When someone puts their selfish reasons above your well-being, they lose the right to stand close to it.

Friendship requires honesty, care, and respect. Once betrayal enters, those things can't survive. What grows instead is something false.

And you don't need that in your life.

Hidden Cost of Loyalty

I carried your secrets like they were my own. When your words bent the truth, I patched them together so others would see only the version of you they wanted to admire. I guarded your image while my own voice went unheard. The price was heavy. I learned to smile through humiliation, bury my anger under silence, and accept pain as if it were the natural cost of being friends with you. Protecting you meant abandoning myself. I did it so often that I forgot what it felt like to be safe. Now I see it for what it was.

Friendship should never ask one person to shrink so the other can shine. It should not demand silence to cover lies or fear to keep peace. What I called loyalty was just submission dressed as devotion, and I stayed tied to someone who thrived on taking everything I cared for most. The chain is broken now. The past is closed. I don't owe you the shield I once held for you.

What I owe is to myself: honesty, respect, and the freedom to walk away from anything that pretends to be friendship but is not.

I Don't Wish You Well

Some people don't deserve closure.

Closure is not a reward I hand out to soothe your conscience. It is not my job to stitch together the holes you left behind or make your story feel complete. Some endings remain jagged, just as some doors stay slammed. This isn't bitterness or revenge; I outgrew you. And when I outgrow something, I don't shrink myself to make it fit again or let nostalgia trick me into repeating mistakes. Some people imagine they're owed closure. They aren't. Closure is a kindness, and I don't owe you kindness. Not anymore. Not after what you did. My growth means I see you for what you were, and I no longer need it. I walk away without leaving a note or the comfort of letting you believe you still matter.

You don't. You're irrelevant.

So no, I don't wish you well. I'm not granting access, giving blessings, or folding the chapter neatly so you can sleep at night. What you get is the truth: you will never matter here again, not in my mind, not in my story, not in the smallest shadow of my future. You don't get a clean goodbye. You get erased.

Time Erased You

Today, I am sad in a way that is hard to put into words. It crept in without warning. I do not know the moment you slipped away, or the point when you stopped mattering. All I know is that time began its slow erasure, and you started to become faceless. I search my memory for your voice, but it feels like chasing echoes down an empty corridor. I know it was once familiar. I used to replay it as easily as a song I could hum without thinking. Now it drifts, thin and unreliable, and I wonder if I am inventing the fragments. Maybe what I hear is only my mind trying to stitch together what no longer lives inside me. Your face is worse.

There was a time I could close my eyes and see you sharply, every feature alive, every angle etched with meaning. Sometimes I catch myself trying to hold outlines, a flicker of your smile, the shadow of your eyes, but the details dissolve like watercolor bleeding across paper.

Now I'm sitting on the edge of my bed, and I think about the way we carry people inside us, how they live there even after they are gone, and how memory shifts under the weight of time. What remains of you in me is only a handful of fragments, and even those are slippery.

That's all that's left for us.

Afraid of the Light

Plato said; We can easily forgive a child who is afraid of the dark. The real tragedy is when men are afraid of the light.

Fear of the dark makes sense when someone is young. A child does not yet know what hides in the shadows. Their imagination fills the unknown with danger. We comfort them and tell them it is all right. We turn on the light to show there is nothing to fear. But what happens when an adult fears the light instead? Not physical light, but truth. Clarity. Honesty. Growth. When someone refuses to face their own flaws. When responsibility is avoided, and ignorance is chosen because facing reality would require change.

A child hides from monsters that are not real. An adult hides from truths that are.

Fear of the dark is natural. Fear of the light is chosen. One comes from innocence. The other from avoidance.

The lesson is simple. Being scared is not a weakness. Staying scared when the truth is right in front of you is that Light may reveal things you do not like. It may uncover mistakes. It may expose lies. Yet it also reveals a possibility. It shows the next step. It offers a way forward. Darkness keeps you frozen. Light sets you in motion.

Love Doesn't Mean Carrying Him

You care about him, but that doesn't make his problems yours. If he refuses to improve his life, that is a decision he is choosing and not one you are meant to fix. Love cannot replace effort, and you should not drain yourself trying to supply what he will not build for himself. You are not his parent or his therapist, and you do not exist to manage a grown man's emotions or responsibilities. Support is healthy, but carrying someone who refuses to walk is not. You have your own life and your own goals, and your time is better used building your future rather than dragging someone toward theirs. If he wants better, he will act like it, and if he does not, then leaving is not cruel; it is self-respect. You are not abandoning him; you are choosing yourself, and that choice is long overdue.

Some Blossoms Must Fade Before Roots Can Grow

At first, I thought I had found the rarest bloom in the garden, the one I would press between the pages of my heart forever. Its petals were bright, its fragrance sweet, and in those early hours, I believed it was love itself. But seasons have their secrets. What I carried so carefully turned out to be only a passing blossom, a brief flare of color that fades when true summer comes. And then, as if the earth had been waiting all along, another flower opened before me, deeper in hue, richer in scent, its roots running farther than I could see. This one was not a fleeting ornament but the soil itself, the kind of growth that teaches you where home is.

It was then I understood: some flowers dazzle, but others hold entire gardens within them.

When She Loves You and When She's Done

A woman in love will move mountains for you. She will defend you, support you, and stand beside you even when no one else does. She remembers the small things you forget. She will wake up early, stay up late, and give more than she ever says out loud. But there is something people do not warn you about. That same woman, if she ever reaches the point where she removes you from her heart, will not look back, argue, or seek revenge. She will definitely not beg you to understand what you lost. She will simply be done.

And when a woman is done, she is done for good.

It is a simple disconnection. She no longer feels anything where you used to live inside her. Your name becomes just another word. Your voice no longer has power. Your stories no longer matter. Even if the world expects her to mourn you, she will not. You were already buried the day she stopped caring. People think strength is loud. Sometimes it is a woman sitting in silence while others expect tears, but she gives none. They do not understand that she already grieved while you were still alive.

By the time you are gone, she has nothing left to feel.

You're Not Failing

I know life has been heavy for you lately. It seems like nothing lines up, like each step just brings another setback. That voice inside keeps saying you're not enough. But hold on. This will not last forever. Things will settle into place, and you'll see that you were never failing. You were just carrying more than most people could.

This world is brighter with you here. You bring more than you know. And never forget, you're extraordinary.

Conversations That Cannot Grow

Not every discussion is worth having. Some conversations are less about the subject itself and more about the readiness of the people involved. Before responding, ask yourself whether the other person has developed the openness to recognize that reality can be seen through more than one lens, that two people can stand in the same moment and see it differently without either being wrong. Instead of clarity, you end up circling the same points, repeating truths that won't be heard.

That's the moment when you need to step back. It does not erase your perspective or silence your voice. To step back in such times is simply choosing to save your energy for places where real exchange can take root. In the end, what matters is knowing where your energy belongs.

Before Anger Turns Me Into Someone Else

Anger takes over fast. It changes the tone of a room and the tone inside your head. I know what it can turn me into if I let it take control. But before it reaches that point, I step back. Not to avoid the problem or to make others comfortable. I do it to protect myself. I would rather walk away with my self-respect than stay and become someone I regret being. Leaving is not defeat. It is prevention. A way to end a moment before it turns into damage. I don't owe anyone an angry version of me.

I don't owe myself that either.

So no, I am not afraid of anger. I am afraid of the version of myself it wakes up.

Trust Isn't a Game

Some people will look you directly in the eye and lie without hesitation, then act offended when you decide you can no longer trust them. They expect you to move forward as if nothing happened, still offering them the benefit of the doubt. Yet every lie leaves a mark, and piece by piece the foundation of honesty begins to crumble. That is why trust does not vanish on its own. It is destroyed, and once that happens, the one who caused the damage has no right to blame you when you choose to walk away.

Gift of Their Absence

Nothing compares to the moment when those who abandoned you begin searching for an excuse to return. At first, they turned away when your presence no longer served their needs, leaving you to carry your struggles alone. They assumed you'd stay in that place of loss, waiting for them to come back. Yet time does not pause for the one who has been left behind. Absence reshapes you. It teaches you how to stand on your own. And then comes the moment when they reappear. Their return is not rooted in loyalty but in curiosity, regret, or even envy of the strength you found without them. They circle back, looking for a way into the very life they dismissed, hoping you will forget the weight of their departure.

But you remember. You remember the silence, the distance, and the sharp edge of being abandoned. That memory is what makes their reappearance so striking. The satisfaction lies not in revenge, but in recognition. You have grown in the space they left behind. You no longer need their approval, nor their presence, to feel whole. And when they try to step back into your story, you see the truth with clarity: that absence was a gift, for it allowed you to build a life stronger than anything you shared when they were still near.

Never the Same

Unfortunately, I am not the person I once was. Life has reshaped me, carving its lessons into every part of who I am. The experiences I have lived, especially the painful ones, have altered the way I carry myself and the way I see the world. When someone chooses to cause harm, it leaves more than a scar. It changes the way I see them, and that change cannot be reversed. Trust, once broken, does not return to its former state. Neither apologies nor time have the power to restore what was lost. The eyes that once looked with openness now see through the filter of what has been done. This isn't resentment. It's self-respect. It means honoring the truth of what happened and protecting yourself with the wisdom pain has given. I keep moving forward, not chained to the past, but strengthened by what it taught me. And though I live with grace, I will never see those who wronged me in the same way again.

The Version of Me That Settled Is Gone

When I look back, I can hardly believe how much I tolerated just to keep certain people in my life. I accepted silence when I deserved answers. I excused disrespect and called it patience. I poured effort into people who gave nothing back and stayed quiet whenever I felt hurt because I did not want to start a conflict. I shrank myself so others could stay comfortable.

That version of me is gone.

I used to think keeping people meant I was strong, loyal, and understanding. Now I see that half of what I called loyalty was fear.

Fear of being alone, misunderstood, and labeled as difficult. But I have learned something important. Losing people who do not value you is not a loss. It is freedom. It clears space for people who see you clearly. It gives you back the time and peace you spent trying to prove your worth to people who never deserved it. I will never betray myself like that again. Choosing myself is not selfish. Respect will be the bare minimum. Effort will be mutual. Peace will not be begged for. If someone requires me to dim who I am to keep them close, I will let them go. The old me chased people. The new me attracts what matches my worth.

End of Illusions

I remember the lies you told and the betrayal that followed. You hurt me even when you didn't have to, and that truth has stayed with me. For a long time, I tried to make sense of it. I told myself stories that might lessen the sting. I convinced myself you didn't mean it, that one day you would change, or that somehow the fault was mine. But the reality is clear: people only change if they choose to, and you never did. In the past, I gave more grace than was deserved. I wanted to believe there was something better in you, that your actions were not the sum of who you were. Over time, though, I saw the pattern for what it was. The disrespect wasn't a slip or a moment of weakness; it was a choice you made again and again. That recognition left me with no illusions, and because of that, there is no place for you in my life ever again.

Beyond Apologies

At first, it feels natural to ask why someone continues to cause harm, but life teaches you a different lesson. In the beginning, you want to understand, wondering if the pain is accidental, if circumstances explain the behavior, or if perhaps one day things will change. Those questions seem necessary, as though answers might soften the hurt. But with time, the truth becomes clear: repeated actions are not accidents, and the explanations you're waiting for will never come. Maturity is recognizing that the cycle will not break simply because you want it to. Patterns reveal themselves, and once you see them clearly, there is no mystery left. Your need for confrontation fades. You stop asking for apologies or explanations. You no longer wait for promises or cling to the hope of something different. Instead, you protect your peace and step away.

A Halo Doesn't Erase the Dirt

A liar is still a liar, even after they start speaking softly and acting honest. A cheater is still a cheater, even if they suddenly show up behaving politely and pure. People like that are often skilled at changing how they present themselves, but not who they truly are. One day they deceive you, then the next they act like a saint, as if a calm voice and a clean image can erase what they did. It does not work like that.

Someone who broke trust does not get to decide when the past disappears. They may pretend to be wiser now. But none of that erases the choices they made or the pain they caused.

Real change is not a performance. Someone who truly regrets their actions doesn't act well for an audience. If someone only became kind after being caught, that is not change, that is damage control.

A liar can memorize honesty. A cheater can rehearse loyalty.

Watch who they are when no one is watching, how they treat people who have nothing to offer them. That will tell you everything.

Because no matter how holy they act now, the stain of who they were doesn't just fade away. Dirt like that doesn't wash off. It only hides until it rains.

She Belongs to Me

I know who I am. I live in this body every day. I know its shape, its changes, and the marks left behind. Life altered me, and I am still learning how to belong within the result. There is still softness here, and I do not deny it. But admitting that doesn't give anyone permission to judge it. I do not want commentary disguised as kindness, especially from those who remember the years I spent trying to vanish. I let others define my value once, and I will not hand it over again. I am not the polished image that lives online. I do not compete with it, and I do not measure myself against it. What I carry may not stand out in a lineup, but I will not apologize for existing outside a standard I never agreed to. If my appearance does not fit what someone wants, they are free to go. But they do not get to wound me on the way out. Cruelty is not a clean exit.

I am imperfect, but I claim this version of myself.

She belongs to me.

Exposed by Your Own Hands

You hurt her and then tried to flip the story when she walked away. The moment she chose herself, you played the victim, pretending her boundaries were harsh while your cruelty was just a mistake. That's how you kept control, by twisting the truth until it made you look small and her look harsh. But the truth is simple: you never wanted accountability. Owning what you did would have forced you to face yourself, and you weren't willing to do that.

So you hid behind lies. You used her pain like a shield, bending it into something you could use for sympathy. You denied the wounds you caused and explained away the scars you left. You thought her honesty would undo her. You believed showing her pain would strip her of dignity. You treated her openness as weakness, assuming it would be the thing that broke her. But you were wrong. Because cruelty doesn't stay hidden. Manipulation always unravels. And when it does, the truth is louder than the story you spun. In trying to break her, you revealed yourself.

What you meant to use against her became the proof of who you really are and who she no longer wants to carry.

No Longer Mistaking Shadows for Light

You and your surroundings taught me a lesson I did not want but needed. Not everyone comes into your life with honesty, truth, or care. Some arrive only to take, kindness worn like a mask. Others stand close, not to support you but to watch how you handle the fall they helped set up. For a long time, I treated presence as proof of loyalty and effort as sincerity. I trusted without question and assumed good intention was natural. That mistake cost me peace. Now I understand that trust is not freely given. It is earned. Proximity does not equal integrity. Some people belong at a distance until their actions prove otherwise. The realization hardened me, but it also freed me. Once you accept that not every shadow is light, you stop handing out your faith to anyone standing nearby.

Fresh Hands and Familiar Corners

A familiar proverb teaches that a new broom sweeps clean, but an old broom knows the corners. It's a simple way of saying that both new strength and long experience have their place. When something is fresh, it comes with energy. A new broom cuts through dust with speed, the same way a new person brings drive and eagerness to prove themselves. That spark can make quick changes and set things in motion. But the broom that's been used for years has its own worth. Its bristles may be worn, yet it knows the hidden spots where dirt gathers. In the same way, someone who has been around longer sees what others overlook. They understand the small details, the hard lessons, and the places that need steady care. This saying reminds us that both sides matter. Fresh energy can get the job started, but lasting wisdom knows how to finish it well.

Dragged Down in Return

Some of us kept others from drowning, and got dragged down in return. We carried people through storms they thought would end them. Sat by their side when no one else did. Took calls in the middle of the night, kept secrets that weren't ours to hold, gave pieces of ourselves that couldn't be replaced. For a while, it feels like strength, like proof that we can handle anything. But the cost comes slow. The more you pour out, the less there is left. You wake up one day and realize your own lungs are burning, and no one is reaching for you. It's a cruel exchange: the people you once kept alive don't always see when you start sinking. They just keep standing on your shoulders while you go under. There's no poetry in it when it happens. Just the silence of knowing you saved someone else at the expense of yourself.

This Is What They Don't Get

They looked at me and said,

"Don't you feel lonely, living in your own little world all the time?"

And I didn't answer right away.

Because it's not a little world to me, it's the only one where I can actually breathe.

Where I don't have to explain myself or shrink just to be tolerated. Where I can think without being corrected, rest without being judged, and exist without always performing for someone else's comfort.

So I looked back and said,

"You mean the world where people pretend all day?

Where you say you're fine when you're not?

Where everything depends on being liked, accepted, and approved?

You think I should trade peace for that? I don't feel lonely in here.

I feel safe.

But maybe that's the part you don't understand, because you've spent so long adjusting yourself for everyone else, you forgot what it's like to just be."

Borrowed Skin

Getting older is something many people don't want to face. Some fight against it with everything they have. They cling to what still shines, to what reminds them of when they were noticed, admired, or feared. They wear the same expressions, tell the same stories, hold on to the same pride. It isn't about playing roles; it is about trying to show themselves and others that they haven't been passed by youth.

But the truth can't be hidden. Time doesn't stop just because someone refuses to admit it. It shows in the face, in the hands, in the voice. No matter how tightly they hold on, the years keep moving. Old habits and bought shine cannot cover for long what time has already claimed. There is something both heartbreaking and deeply human in this struggle, the need to stay important, to be remembered as they once were, to resist the fact of change. But the world does not pause for anyone. Nobody wants to believe their young days are gone. Pretending does not change reality.

And what they forget is this: beauty was never in borrowed skin. It's in what time can't steal.

The Echo of Who You Were

You play the role they pay you for. The costume fits, though it is stitched from fabric that never feels like your own skin. Each word spoken on that stage is measured, rehearsed, crafted for an audience that wants a performance, not the real you. So you bow on cue, as expected, and the applause comes crashing like a storm. Louder, brighter, emptier than anything you once believed applause could mean. The crowd does not see the silence inside you. They see only the mask, the practiced smile, the way you hold your shoulders, like a script has already been written. Their approval is a currency, their cheers a contract, and you sign it with the parts of yourself you can never reclaim.

And when the lights dim, and the curtains close, there is nothing left but the echo of a name you once stood tall behind. A faint memory of the self you traded for the security of benefit and the shallow promise of recognition. In that hollow quiet, the stage is stripped bare, and so are you. The truth is, you sell more than your labor. You sell the voice that could speak freely, the strength that could choose differently. You let it slip away, piece by piece, until applause becomes more important than authenticity, and coin more sacred than meaning. And though the audience leaves, satisfied with the show, you remain behind with the truth: that the role you play may be bought, but the cost is everything you once swore you would never give away.

New Shrink to Fit
(and Other Tragedies in My Closet)

Maybe that's where it started. That exact moment when I decided love was something you earned by disappearing. Not all at once, obviously. I'm far too dramatic for a clean exit. No, I chose the slow dissolve.

The elegant vanishing act. Think Houdini, but with better hair and more emotional damage. I trimmed parts of myself like a bad haircut, fully convinced I needed to shed my personality for others' sake.

So I dimmed, edited, filtered, smiled on cue, and clapped politely for mediocrity, all while folding myself into progressively smaller versions of a girl who once had opinions, dreams, and a smile that startled people at restaurants. The girl who wanted her partner to be with her at the top, not stuck with the same ol' same old miserableness.

So I wore shoes that didn't fit, jeans that couldn't possibly be meant for human thighs, and expectations that should've come with a warning label and a bottle of tequila. Ideally served at the table where I was never even seated, while they framed the mess and blamed the mirror.

Apparently, I triggered some sort of group crisis with my existence.

But that's not a me problem. That's a them and their carefully curated, fake-smiling, gossip-powered ecosystem problem.

The kind where backstabbing counts as bonding and accountability is considered an attack. Looking back, I can't tell if I was trying to be lovable or simply trying to be less offensive to anyone with eyeballs and an opinion. Probably both. But what I do know is this: if someone only loves the version of me that's been downsized, muted, and dipped in vanilla, then they're not loving me.

They're loving a mannequin. And mannequins, as we all know, are terrible conversationalists.

So, no more shrink-wrapping my soul to fit inside someone else's comfort zone.

I am a puppet to no one. Not for love, not for money, not for favor. If I'm too much, then maybe they're just not enough.

And honestly? That sounds like a them problem.

They've got to live with themselves.

I already did the hard part, surviving them.

Failure Isn't Final

Failure isn't final. It's a floor, not a coffin. You can stand on it, climb from it, and use it. Loss is often treated as the end of the road, a verdict on who someone is and what they can become. But it is not a burial ground. It does not close the story. It simply turns the page. A fall is not erasure but a new surface: solid ground that proves life goes on. That low place brings perspective. From there, hidden details come into view. Things once overlooked come to light. Moving forward from that place shapes a person in ways success never could. Setbacks do not define a life. They prepare it. They offer footing for what comes next.

When Grief Outlives Support

Grief is strange because it feels like your whole world has stopped, yet everything around you keeps moving. Stores stay open. People go to work. Traffic still piles up in the morning.

Life carries on as if nothing happened.

At first, people call. They send messages. They tell you to reach out if you need anything. You say thank you, even though you do not know what you need. Then slowly, the messages stop. The calls fade.

No one checks in anymore. Their lives return to normal. Yours does not. You are left with a hurt that does not clock out.

You wake up with it, carry it through the day, and go to bed with it.

Some days you hold it together. Some days you do not. What people do not understand is that grief does not end when support ends. It does not stop when others stop noticing. It lingers long after the flowers wilt and the words "stay strong" are no longer said.

If you are in that place where everything feels broken, and no one is watching anymore, it does not mean you are failing. It means you are human. It means you are still loving someone who is no longer here, or mourning something you lost that others have already moved on from. You should not have to rush your healing just because the world moved on. Grief is not on a schedule.

And even if the world forgets, your pain still matters.

Celebrate Tiny Things

A good coffee, a song that hits right, a smile in the street. Stack those small sparks; they add up fast.

Life is often measured in milestones, the big markers that seem to define progress. But the truth is, most days are made from fragments. Small encounters. Fleeting comforts. The overlooked details that never make it into a headline but hold us together when everything feels thin. So stack them, collect them, and let them count. They are not fillers between the big events; they are the substance of living. Celebrate tiny things. They are the sparks that keep the fire alive.

Laugh at Mistakes

Messed up? Good.

That means you tried. Laugh, learn, keep rolling. Mistakes are not a weakness. They are signs of movement. Each one shows you stepped beyond the safe zone, stretched further than comfort allowed. A mistake can sting, but it does not need to be a wound. Humor softens, time reframes, and practice builds skill. What feels awkward today can shape you tomorrow. So laugh at mistakes. They show you are alive, active, and still in the game.

Keep Curiosity Alive

Ask what if? More often. It keeps life fresh.

Curiosity opens doors that routine would leave closed. It makes the familiar look new and the expected less certain. A single question can shift the way you see a problem, a place, or even yourself. When curiosity fades, life shrinks. Days feel narrow, choices feel fixed. But when you let yourself wonder, even simple things carry possibility.

Forgive Yourself

Forgive yourself for the blindness that led you into the path of betrayal. You could not have known the mask someone else chose to wear. You trusted because your heart was open, and that openness is not a fault. A good heart does not always recognize the shadow in another. It sees what is possible, it believes in light, hopes, and honesty. There is no shame in that. Do not turn against yourself for the harm done by another hand. Hold to the truth that your goodness was never a mistake.

Boundaries Make You the Villain

Lately, I've noticed something. The more I stand up for myself, the more I look like the problem. When I let things slide, people liked me. I was agreeable, easy, and safe. I didn't push back. I tolerated the comments. Kept the peace, even when it cost me. But now I draw lines. Suddenly, I'm falling out with people. Called difficult. Told I'm the one "changing." What's really happening isn't that I've become the villain. It's that people are finally hearing no. And some don't like it. Boundaries are not punishment. It's self-respect. Which draws the line between being treated however someone wants and saying, "That doesn't work anymore." So I stopped staying silent. And when I did, it became clear who had benefited most from it. They were never at ease with respect, only with advantage.

Once that ended, so did their comfort.

Dust Settles After the Storm

It was a year like no other. A year of extreme chaos and calm, heartbreak and healing, losing things that felt permanent, and gaining what was never expected but deeply needed. Life flipped itself inside out. Yet, in the middle of it all, something began to shift. Forced to look inward, to face what had been avoided for too long. Then the rebuilding began, piece by piece.

There were moments that cracked everything open, and moments that proved strength was still there. Some people came, left a bitter taste, and nothing but lessons. A few stayed long enough to remind us what safety and warmth feel like. Some choices were made in a rush. Others, after long nights awake. At first, they brought fear, but over time, they revealed their purpose.

And then, unexpectedly, new people appeared. They didn't erase the past, but their presence changed everything that followed. They brought calm where there had been restlessness, and without even knowing, they brought laughter and happiness back into rooms that had gone quiet. After all the breaking, something beautiful took its place. Things didn't just settle; they transformed, and this time, it really seems for the better.

So here is to the moment everything shifted and the feeling of being ready for the new beginning.

Goodbye to what was. And a full-hearted hello to everything that's still to come.

What is a trauma bond?

People think it's love, but it's not.

It's survival. It's what happens when the person who broke you is also the person your body believes will keep you safe. It doesn't make sense in your head, but your heart and your nervous system don't care about logic. They care about patterns and what feels familiar, even when familiar is painful. You stayed, not because you didn't know it hurt, but leaving felt worse. And the silence that came after felt louder than the fights ever did. You forgave things you swore you'd never forgive. You told yourself it wasn't that bad, made excuses, because admitting the truth meant starting over, and you were already so tired. You called it love because calling it what it really was would've shattered you. Loyalty to pain is not loyalty at all. It is captivity.

Box of Darkness

Now and then, someone we care about hands us something we never wanted: pain, loss, or disappointment. At first, it feels like cruelty. It feels like we have been left holding a heavy box that we did not ask for, one we do not know how to open or even carry.

When I first heard the words "Someone I loved once gave me a box full of darkness," I thought only of heartbreak.

Darkness seemed like a punishment, a reminder that love can hurt more deeply than anything else. But with time, I began to see it differently. Pain often carries instruction hidden inside it, lessons only visible once the sting fades.

A box of darkness can teach us about the strength we did not know we had. It can show us the edges of who we are and what matters most. It forces us to slow down, to face what is hard, and to ask ourselves: what will I do with this? Sometimes it even opens our eyes to what we had overlooked, the parts of ourselves that can grow even in hard soil. Years later, the box does not look like cruelty anymore. It looks like a strange gift, which can change you from the inside out and teach us wisdom and a deeper sense of compassion.

And that is the moment when we can stand up and say it out loud.

Yes, someone I loved gave me a box full of darkness. It took me years to understand, but now I can see it was a gift.

Love Isn't Always Enough

We grow up hearing that love can fix anything. Movies, songs, and stories promise that if two people truly care, they'll overcome every obstacle. It's a comforting idea, but life often shows something harder: that feeling alone doesn't carry a relationship through. Yet it is powerful, softens anger, makes hard days bearable, and reminds us we're not alone. But it isn't the same as compatibility. Two people can feel deeply connected and still find themselves clashing over money, family, or the way they want to live. It doesn't erase differences in values, nor does it heal wounds that keep reopening. There's also the matter of effort. Without it, even strong affection wears thin. A couple might still care, but if one person feels unheard or unsafe, affection won't erase the damage. Sometimes the hardest truth is this: leaving doesn't mean the love wasn't real, it just wasn't enough to build the life both people needed. That realization hurts, but it also frees us to see that lasting relationships demand more than feelings. They rest on communication, patience, and shared direction. Love is still with us at the end of it all.

But it doesn't build a home. That part is ours.

When Love Becomes a Bargain, Nobody Really Wins

Some people treat love like a business deal. They measure what they're getting: status, comfort, money, or security. To them, it's the advantages that matter. So they never really get cheated. If all they want is gain, then gain is all they'll ever have. When those things fade or get taken away, there's nothing lasting left. You can't call it a loss if you never cared about what was priceless. On the other hand, love isn't about lists or roles. It's about connection, choosing someone, and being chosen back. When that's replaced with material things, the heart stays empty. So if someone turns away from love for something shinier, let them.

They're not being robbed, they're simply getting what they bargained for, and missing the only treasure that lasts.

Attention or Respect?

The Difference That Changes Everything

We live in a world where attention feels like currency.

The likes, the views, the applause. We chase them, often without even noticing how much of ourselves we give away in the process. It feels good in the moment, like a spark. But sparks fade. Attention doesn't last. It moves on to the next face, the next voice, the next trend. And if all we've built ourselves on is the flicker of being noticed, we'll always end up hungry again. Respect is different. It doesn't just glance at you. It grounds itself in who you are, what you stand for, and how you carry yourself when no one's clapping.

Think of it like this: attention is someone admiring your outfit. Respect is someone trusting your word. One is surface. The other is substance. Respect isn't loud or instant, but it stays. People might forget what you posted, but they remember how you treated them. They might scroll past your photo, but they'll hold onto the way you showed up when it counted.

When you realize that difference, you stop starving for applause or measuring your worth by how many people are watching. Instead, you start living in a way that deserves respect.

Attention is nice. Respect is necessary. One can make you feel seen for a while. The other makes you feel solid forever.

I Needed Him to Break Me to Finally Walk Away

I used to wonder why I kept returning to someone I knew would only hurt me. On the surface, it made no sense. Friends would tell me I deserved better, and deep down I knew they were right. But the truth is, going back wasn't about believing this would change. It was the opposite. Every time I returned, it was like pressing on a bruise. The pain needed to grow so sharp, so unbearable, that one day it couldn't be touched again. I wanted him to hurt me so badly that whatever feelings were left would finally burn away.

And that's exactly what happened. In the very last week I was with him, he told me something terrible he had done. I don't mean he cheated or something like that. That already happened, as other people were so kind as to tell me. This was far worse. That's when my love dried up, and the hope that used to pull me back was gone. That awful, disgusting truth brought me to the only place where I could walk away from him without turning back, ever.

It killed every single excuse I had left.

PS

Sometimes people think healing means protecting themselves from more pain, but for me, it meant stepping into it until there was nothing left to feel. It wasn't pretty, and most definitely not what anyone would call healthy, but it was real. And in the end, he's the one who will live with the shame that set me free.

Lonely Hurt

One of the worst feelings is when your heart suddenly feels heavy for no clear reason. It hits out of nowhere. You try to breathe through it, but it sits in your chest like a weight you cannot lift. You think about reaching out, but no one feels close enough. So you sit there in silence. Tears come, even when you try to stop them. You grab your chest like you are trying to hold yourself together. You pray the pain will fade, or at least slow down long enough for you to catch your breath.

This kind of hurt does not come from one moment. It builds slowly through held-in words, swallowed emotions, and all the times you pretended to be fine when you were not. Eventually, the body lets it out for you. People assume the worst pain comes from being hurt by someone else. But sometimes the real pain comes from having no one to turn to when you are hurting. That loneliness cuts deeper than any insult or betrayal. Nothing anyone says fixes it in the moment. All you can do is remind yourself that the feeling will pass, even if it does not feel like it right now. You may be crying alone, but you are still surviving it.

And sometimes, that is proof enough that you are stronger than you think.

Why We Keep Trying to Fix What's Already Broken

People don't let go easily. When something breaks, whether a relationship, a dream, or a part of ourselves, we hold on, even when it hurts. We keep trying because it mattered, and walking away feels like erasing all the time, energy, and love we poured into it. Sometimes it is guilt. If we just try harder, maybe we can undo the damage. Other times, it is a habit. We live with something so long that letting go feels like losing a part of who we are.

But more often, it is fear. The unknown weighs heavier than the pain we already know. At the heart of it all, we are searching for meaning. If we can repair what's broken, we can prove it was not all for nothing. Even when logic says it's over, our hearts still reach for another chance. The truth is, not everything can be fixed. And the longer we try, the more we risk breaking ourselves instead. Yet those attempts are not wasted. They prove the depth of love, hope, and the refusal to let losses define us.

How Strange Is Man

It's a funny thing about people. We spend so much of our time caught between three places: the past, the present, and the future. And most of the time, we're not even living in the one we're actually in. Think about it. Someone is sitting in the middle of their life right now, maybe with a job, maybe with a family, maybe just trying to figure it all out. But instead of living that moment, they're busy worrying about what comes next. Will I make enough money? Will I find love? Will tomorrow look like today? And while the mind sprints toward tomorrow, the present is burning away. What could've been laughter turns into stress. What could've been a memory turns into a missed chance.

Then, when the future finally arrives and becomes the new "today," it doesn't feel like a gift. It feels like regret. That same person looks back at the days they once ignored and suddenly wishes they could go back. They sit in tomorrow, crying over yesterday, replaying old moments, holding on to memories like souvenirs from a trip they didn't realize was ending. It's strange. People keep destroying the present while chasing the future, then ruining the future by dragging the past into it. They run in circles, never fully here, never fully there.

Friendships Fade

Not every friendship ends with a blow-up or some big, dramatic fight. A lot of the time, it's softer than that. The texts come less often, calls stop, and the energy shifts. What once felt like home just doesn't feel the same anymore. And that's not a bad thing. People change. You do, and so do they. Sometimes the version of you that once fit perfectly with someone just isn't there now. That doesn't make the friendship any less real or meaningful. It just means it had its time. Some people stay for the long run. Others are only here for a season. They show up, bring something important, and then life moves you in different directions. And that's okay. They were never supposed to be the whole story, just a chapter, and a good one. The best part of friendships that fade like this is that there doesn't have to be anger. You can look back without regret and accept it for what it was.

And maybe, somewhere down the road, life will let you meet again, just as different people.

Ending Becomes a Beginning

I used to believe that losing him would be the end of me. But when I finally left, something unexpected happened. I did not fall apart. Instead, I began to rise. I reconnected with the people who mattered. I drew closer to my friends, laughed more, and felt real joy in their company. I also returned to the passions I had abandoned and poured myself into them with fresh energy. The spark I thought was gone came back. My body started to heal. My hair stopped falling out, my skin cleared, and my eyes looked brighter than they had in a long time. I hadn't even realized how much sadness I was carrying until it was gone. The truth is, what we fear losing is often the very thing holding us back. The ending I once dreaded became the beginning of a stronger, brighter version of myself.

And if I could find that strength, so can you.

Opposition Reveals Belief

"Why would those who doubt you, block you, or criticize you, secretly be the ones who believe in your strength?"

At first, that feels upside down. Yet, if you look closer, it makes sense. No one fights a battle they think is already lost. We see this everywhere. In history, powerful movements always attracted the harshest resistance. The louder the voices for change became, the stronger the forces that rose to silence them. The resistance itself revealed the truth: people knew change was possible, and that frightened them.

The same happens in personal life. Maybe it's a friend who distances themselves when you start to grow, or a partner who resists your new direction. Even jealous family members. They are the worst. Their pushback is often less about you being weak and more about them knowing you might outgrow the space they are comfortable in.

And here is the strange part: opposition is often a backhanded compliment. Indifference is the real insult. Of course, that does not mean it feels good. Resistance can feel heavy, lonely, even confusing. But with distance, you can see it for what it is: a form of recognition. People don't ignore you unless you carry enough strength to unsettle them.

That is the hidden mirror inside opposition. It shows you what others already see: that you are far more powerful than you thought.

You cannot be bought. They can.

Forgive, But Don't Forget

I'm a forgiving person. I own my mistakes, say sorry when I'm wrong, and believe in giving people a fair chance. That is who I am, and I don't apologize for it.

But forgiveness is not unlimited access. If someone crosses me once, I take note. Twice, and I start protecting myself. I won't act like nothing happened or hand out free chances to someone who keeps proving they don't deserve them.

Hurt me, and I will create distance. I choose people who match my effort. I don't hold grudges, but I remember patterns. I protect my peace and move forward with those who know what respect looks like. Being forgiving is a strength. So is refusing to be mistreated. I forgive. I learn. I walk away when I need to. That is my balance.

Givers and Takers

There are two kinds of people: givers and takers.

Givers enter a room and bring light with their care. They give what they have, even when it costs them deeply. They know the weight of sacrifice, and they carry it without asking for applause. Takers drain the air. They lean on every shoulder, pull from every hand, and call it love when it is only using others for their gain. They appear only when they want something. The rest of the time, you would not even know they existed. The cruelest part is that they believe this is enough.

The truth is clear. Givers build the ground beneath us. They stand with love that outlasts their years. Takers strip it bare. They end with no pride, still pretending to hold value, demanding respect they never earned, revealed as the frauds they always were.

Fading

I started to forget your voice. Not all at once, but in fragments. The way it was carried at the end of a sentence. The pause before you laughed. The sound when you were tired. I reach for it in my mind, and it is no longer there the way it once was. Your face is fading, too. When I close my eyes, it does not appear as it used to. Sometimes I catch the outline, the curve of your smile, the sharpness of your eyes, but never the whole of you. It is like looking at a photograph left too long in the sun, familiar but faint. It does not frighten me. It shows me what forgetting looks like. How someone once held so tightly can vanish in slow motion until nothing remains but the reminder that they are no longer worth remembering.

Collaboration Beats Competition

Many people grow up believing success is something you win by defeating others. That thinking creates constant comparison and insecurity. It keeps people focused sideways instead of forward. The people who truly rise do not waste time trying to outdo everyone around them. They learn from others, share ideas, and build connections. They understand that helping someone advance does not set them back. It strengthens their position.

Collaboration opens doors that competition cannot. One person alone has limited information, limited reach, and limited perspective. Working with others multiplies knowledge, support, and opportunity. Progress is not about beating the person next to you. It is about surrounding yourself with people who lift you, and becoming someone who lifts others in return.

Power of Standing Apart

People often mistake staying to yourself as weakness, as if it means you don't belong or you're too closed off to connect. But that's not the truth at all. Choosing to step back isn't about being a loner. It is actually valuing yourself enough to protect your energy. When you don't jump into every crowd, you give yourself the chance to see things clearly. You notice who's genuine and who's just putting on a show. You realize how much of what goes on around you is just noise, loud, messy, attention-seeking noise. That's when you learn that you don't have to be part of it. That choice takes strength. It's not easy to stand apart when the world pushes you to join in, to perform, to play along. But strength isn't always about being the loudest voice in the room. Sometimes it's about having the courage to stay grounded in yourself, to say,

"I know who I am, and I don't need to prove it by being part of the circus."

Cheating Is Easy

Try Something More Challenging, Like Being Faithful

Anybody can cheat. It doesn't take talent, courage, or strength. It's just giving in to the first temptation that comes along. Taking the shortcut, thinking nobody will notice, convincing yourself you deserve it, or that it's harmless. But the truth is, cheating is easy because it asks nothing of you. No courage, no commitment, nothing to stand up for. It's the lazy road, the fast fix, the escape hatch. Cheating might give you a rush, an ego boost. But it robs you, too. It takes away your integrity, your ability to look someone in the eye without shame. Or, most of the time, some people don't feel shame at all. For them, it's normal. Being faithful, that's the real challenge. It means choosing the same person every single day, even when life gets hard, your feelings shift, or distractions show up waving their hands in front of you. Deciding to stay when you could run, and love when it isn't convenient. Faithfulness isn't glamorous. It doesn't always get applause. Some days it's just two people deciding to show up for each other in the middle of arguments, disappointments, or long silences. It's carrying responsibility and still choosing closeness. It's listening when you'd rather tune out and honesty when lies might smooth things over. And here's the thing, faithfulness is showing and saying, "I promised you I'd be here, and I still am." Trying again after you've hurt each other, making repairs instead of excuses, and letting trust grow one decision at a time. But there are times when dishonesty keeps stacking up, when stories twist further from the truth, and betrayal tears through the foundation. When that happens, love can't hold, and the only choice left is to walk away.

What Defines a Real Man?

Some men measure their worth by how many women they can get attention from. They see it as proof that they are desirable or important. That kind of behavior often shows insecurity more than strength.

A mature man does not need constant validation from multiple women. Instead, he chooses one partner and puts his energy into building a stable and supportive relationship. That focus creates a solid foundation not just for the relationship but for personal growth, family life, and long-term goals.

Jumping from woman to woman is not power. It only shows that he is weak, destructive, and forgettable. In the end, the only thing he proves is that he cannot build anything that lasts.

Not Everyone Can Be Your Friend

There is a saying that a friend to all is a friend to none. It sounds harsh at first, but it makes sense when you think about it. Real friendship requires loyalty, honesty, and effort. You cannot give that to everyone. If someone claims to be close with everybody, it usually means they are not truly loyal to anyone.

Choose Where Your Energy Goes

Every day, people run into things that test their patience. Someone cuts in line, traffic slows to a crawl, a message gets left on read, or a co-worker makes a small mistake. These moments feel annoying in real time, but most of them will not matter tomorrow. Think about the last week. How many times did you get upset at something small, only to forget about it the next day? That shows how temporary most frustrations are. Yet in the moment, they can eat away at your energy and leave you feeling drained.

The real cost of irritation is not the event itself, but the way it shapes your mindset. This is where choice comes in. You can decide not to hand over control of your mood to minor problems. That does not require pretending nothing bothers you. It simply asks you to draw a line between what deserves your focus and what does not. If something will matter in a week, a month, or a year, then it is worth attention. But if it will be gone from memory by tomorrow, it does not deserve to take up space in your day.

Belonging Has a Place

Accepting people for who they are is an essential part of living well. Everyone carries their own story, habits, and personality. Trying to reshape them into your version of "right" only creates frustration. Peace comes when you stop fighting against reality, but that doesn't mean everyone should hold the same place in your life. People show who they are through action, not intention. A friend who breaks promises can still be treated with courtesy, but they shouldn't be the one you depend on during a crisis. A person who proves reliable earns a closer place.

This isn't about judgment; it's about clarity. Placing people where they belong keeps life balanced. It protects your energy, spares you from misplaced expectations, and makes room for those who bring honesty and care.

Losing Your Place

When you decide to ignore her, you might think you're making her struggle, that she'll feel your absence so strongly she'll come back desperate for your attention. The truth is different. Distance doesn't weaken her; it teaches her. She adjusts to the silence, learns to hold her own feelings. Life doesn't pause. It continues without you. What you don't see is that your silence also changes the place you hold. Every day removes you from her world. And soon, your place will be given to someone better.

Realness Is Louder Than Performance

Everything you do for attention is the reason why you do not have mine. When someone is always showing off, bragging, or seeking validation, it becomes clear that they are acting for approval instead of living with purpose. There is no peace in constantly performing.

Illusion of Being Above

When a woman who knows her worth calls a man toward his potential, what she sees in him, she exposes the cracks in his character. Instead of rising to the challenge, he retreats. Strength requires growth, accountability, and resilience, qualities he may lack or refuse to develop. Rather than facing himself, he seeks comfort in the arms of someone who asks less of him. A low-value woman becomes his refuge because she allows him to remain small and gives herself the illusion of being above him. What feels like validation is only a reflection of his immaturity. True strength never shrinks to be loved, and true partnership does not run from the weight of responsibility.

What Love Reveals

Someone very close to him said to me months ago, when we were out one evening,

"He's not honest. Always twisting the truth to suit himself. You gave him space to be better, and he couldn't hold it. With you, he was himself. Now, he's not that man anymore. He's smaller, meaner, and it shows. You're way better off without him. Don't ever go back. He'll never give you anything but a story. He's not good for you."

I haven't stopped thinking about it. Not for what it says about him. That part has long passed. What stayed with me was how different someone can become depending on who they're standing next to. The right kind of presence can make someone stop performing. You get to see who they are when they're not hiding.

That's what love does when it's real. Not everyone brings that out in someone else. Some people don't even try. Some settle for performance, usefulness, and compliance. Others believe that's what love is: keeping the mask on so no one sees too much. But when you've given someone a place where they could be unmasked, you see the change once it's gone. You see the dim. You see them straining to look fine, to act fine, when underneath it's clear something has been lost. Maybe that's the hardest part. Not what it says about them, not even what it says about you, but what it reveals about love itself. And sometimes the most powerful thing you can give someone is the freedom to be who they are.

Once they've had that, losing it changes them in ways they cannot hide.

Seeing What People Don't Say

"Listen with your eyes, and you'll see everything you need to hear."

At first glance, the phrase might sound contradictory. Listening is something we're taught to do with our ears. But if you pay attention in daily life, you'll notice how much people communicate without saying a word. Communication isn't just spoken language. A person's posture, facial expression, or even the way they look at you can reveal more than a full conversation.

Someone might say, "I'm fine," but if they avoid eye contact, cross their arms, or hold tension in their shoulders, you know right there something is wrong. Your ears hear the words, but your eyes catch the truth. Listening with your eyes also teaches patience. People aren't always ready to put feelings into words. Not everyone knows how to express what they feel. Some aren't ready, others are afraid. By staying observant, you give them space to be understood without pressure. That's real respect. Seeing not only what is said, but also what is shown.

Running From Yourself Won't Fix Anything

Insecure people switch partners again and again, hoping a new relationship will solve their problems. They blame every breakup on the other person. One was too distant. Another was too controlling. Another was not on their level. Yet the same issues follow them every time. The common factor is not the partners. It is them.

Changing partners is easy. Changing yourself takes real effort. It means admitting fault, facing insecurities, and healing old wounds. It means dealing with patterns instead of hiding behind a fresh start. Many avoid that work. They would rather replace people than fix their habits. A new relationship may feel exciting at first, but eventually the same behaviors rise back up. Dishonesty. Jealousy. Anger. Poor communication. Fear of commitment. Fear of being alone. If those problems are ignored, they always return.

The real upgrade is not finding a better partner. It is becoming a better version of yourself. When you grow, you stop repeating the same relationship. You no longer need to keep replacing people. The right person will match who you truly are, not who you pretend to be.

Trauma Bond

A trauma bond happens when pain and attachment get tangled. You get hurt, but the same person who hurts you is the one you reach for comfort. That cycle can feel like love, but it is really a tie that keeps you stuck. It makes you believe leaving is harder than staying. You tell yourself things will change, or you blame yourself for the damage. That is how the bond keeps pulling you back. The truth is, it is not your fault. And while a trauma bond feels unshakable, it can be broken. The first step is seeing it for what it truly is: control, not love or care. From there, little by little, you can find your way out.

If You Can't Leave for You, Leave for Her

Some people would throw themselves in front of a train for someone they love. No hesitation. Boom. Gone. Not even a second thought. But ask them to leave a toxic relationship for their own mental health, and suddenly it becomes complicated. Reasons appear. History. Guilt. Timing. The dog just got used to the new apartment. The couch is comfortable. They make good pancakes on Sunday. Whatever. If someone treated your best friend like this, you would not hesitate. You would burn their house down with your eyes and salt the ground they walked on. You would show up with wine, snacks, and a whole PowerPoint presentation about why he is garbage. You would scream, cry, block his number yourself, and then take her to a spa. Yet for yourself, you minimize. You hope they will change if you just love them better, softer, smaller. You give them one more chance. Then another. Until it becomes a ritual, a tradition, it is wild how easy it is to pour love into someone else and treat your own needs like an inconvenience. You are not the exception to human dignity. You are not the only person on Earth who must earn the right to be safe. If you cannot do it for yourself yet, fine. Do it for the version of you who still believes in magic, for the kid you used to be, and for the person you will be ten years from now who wakes up and wonders what the hell took so long.

Pack your bag. Block their number. Go. The couch was not that great anyway.

She Stayed Too Long

She thought it was love. That's what she told herself whenever he let her down. When a line was crossed, she always made room for him to return. He didn't hit her. That was what made it harder to explain. His cruelty wasn't the sort people could see. He twisted words until she believed she was the one overreacting.

Whenever she started to pull back, he did just enough to pull her close again. She stayed through things she never thought she'd tolerate. Words that cut her down. Other women. Promises made just to be broken. She carried it all and called it strength. As time went by, she started disappearing in that relationship, bit by bit. Laughter faded. Plans stopped being made. The girl in the mirror was unrecognizable. The face looked old, worn down. Eyes appeared tired even after a full night's sleep. Friends noticed. They asked if she was okay. The answer was always fine. Explaining the sort of heartbreak that happens slowly was impossible.

What broke her in the end wasn't one moment. It was the accumulation of moments left unrepaired. She gave everything she had to someone who took it without thinking. When she finally walked away, it wasn't out of anger. It was exhaustion. She left that relationship carrying more than heartbreak. Forced walls to rise that hadn't been there before. It left her older in a way no one talks about. But one truth remains: she stayed too long.

And it cost her something she'll never fully get back, the time she wasted.

Talk Is Cheap When Actions Don't Match

I once read a quote:

"He was a man of many words, but never a man of his word."

How true it is. He always knew how to talk. Promises came easily to him. He spoke about love, loyalty, and commitment as if he mastered them, but when it came time to prove it, he disappeared. There's a difference between talking like a good person and living like one. Some people use words for comfort, not commitment. They rely on charm instead of character. They think saying something is the same as doing it. A real man does not make loud claims. He shows up. His consistency speaks louder than any speech.

With time, you learn that words without action mean nothing.

I'd rather deal with someone who stays silent and proves themselves than someone who speaks beautifully and delivers nothing. Honesty in silence is better than lies dressed as affection. In the end, talking is easy. Showing up is rare. And that's how you know who's real.

I Gave It Permission

My story. Written as if it were you.

You used to think it was the storm's fault. It blew in, knocked things over, and left the house in disorder. That was the story you told yourself. It felt easier to believe the blame belonged out there, somewhere you couldn't control. But that was never the full truth.

The storm didn't slide the door open. You did. You were the one who made space for it to enter. You let it come inside, and once it was in, it acted the only way it knew how. It's hard to face that. Harder than saying the house was ruined by something strong outside you. Because the beginning was never just the storm. It started with you, choosing to leave the way open.

That's the part you sit with now. Not only the mess that followed, but the fact that you gave it permission to start.

A Canvas of Nothing

I came to understand something I once resisted: there is no spark in you, no hidden fire I missed. For a long time, I thought that was only old hurt speaking, but the longer I sat with it, the clearer it became. You have not once stepped past the ordinary. What you gave was never enough to draw me in fully. I was the one who painted meaning onto scraps, who turned small gestures into signs of promise. My imagination filled the silence with stories. My longing dressed absence as mystery. I saw storms where the air never moved. The truth is, you stayed the same. Nothing. Wasted. More a shadow in the background than a real presence in my life. And still, I called that distance devotion and named that emptiness love.

I Didn't Understand It Until I Faced the Opposite

I did not understand love when I was inside it. I only understood when I met what it was not. The lies. The manipulation. The inconsistency. The temporary affection followed by sudden distance. That was not it. Real love does not confuse you or make you question your worth. It does not make you chase just to feel safe. I used to think it was proven through struggle and pain. Now I know it shows through peace and consistency. Sometimes the best lesson comes from what breaks us, because the pain reveals what we should never again accept in its name.

Letting It Go

By the end, I decided just to let it go. For a long time, I carried it around. An argument, a disappointment, a thought that pressed against me. I replayed it in my head, as if turning it one more time would finally make it lighter. But instead, it held me down, as if I had chosen to live inside the shadow of something already past. I did believe I had to solve it. I kept explaining to myself, rewrite the story, make it end differently. But the truth was, holding on only left me broken.

Then I asked myself: what if I didn't?

What if I set it down and simply walk away from something that no longer belongs to me? So I did. Letting go didn't mean forgetting. It didn't mean erasing what happened or pretending it never hurt. It meant I wasn't going to spend any more of my days tangled in it.

The strange thing is, the moment I loosened my grip, the world felt lighter. I had thought release would feel like loss, but it didn't. It felt like relief.

Fight, Flight, Freeze, or Fawn

People talk about fight or flight as if those are the only ways humans react when they feel threatened. But there are actually four common patterns: fight, flight, freeze, and fawn. These are automatic survival responses. The body and mind pick them up long before a person thinks through what is happening.

A FIGHT can look like anger bursting out, or it can be smaller: raising your voice, setting a hard boundary, saying, "You can't talk to me like that." Some people move toward conflict when they feel cornered.

FLIGHT is the urge to get away. For some, that means literally leaving the room. For others, it is distraction, overworking, staying busy, so there is no space to feel what hurts.

FREEZE happens when the body and mind slam on the brakes. Muscles tense. Thoughts scatter or go blank. Words do not come out. People describe feeling stuck, unable to move, even if they want to.

FAWN (also called appeasement) means pleasing to stay safe. It is softening conflict, easing over tension, keeping others happy, so the threat does not grow. Many who fawn learned early that their safety depended on keeping others calm.

These patterns are not choices at first. They are learned survival strategies, built over time, often in childhood. They can help in the moment, but feel confusing or painful later. The good news is they can be unlearned. It starts by noticing them without shame. Awareness opens the door to choice, and support helps people learn new ways of responding. Ways that fit the present, not the past.

Mine to Release

I forgive you, but understand this forgiveness is not for you, and it does not rewrite what happened. It is my decision to stop carrying what never should have been mine to hold. But here's what you can never escape:

You will never forgive yourself. And that's the part you'll never live with.

You can silence it for a while, drown it in noise, distract yourself with anything that keeps you from looking too closely. Yet it always comes back late at night, when nothing else is there to cover it. You'll walk to the end with the shadow of what you did. And that is going to haunt you beyond that.

Being Alone Starts to Feel Like the Only Safe Option

Being alone doesn't feel like a temporary phase anymore. It starts to feel like the safest choice.

You get older and realize that finding someone solid, someone who actually shows up, stays consistent, and builds with you, isn't as common as it should be. Most folks are lost in their own mess. Some are still chasing old loves. Others are stuck in their ego. And then there are the worst ones, the ones who walk into your life halfway. They won't love you properly, but they also won't let you leave.

That kind of misery hits harder than being alone ever could.

It makes you step back and ask yourself if love is even worth the confusion anymore, if starting over again, opening up again, explaining your heart again is worth the risk of ending up in another almost relationship with someone who only wants you on their terms. Maybe being alone isn't sad. Maybe it's choosing to protect your energy from halfhearted people. Choosing to build a life where you don't have to wonder if you matter, or if someone is only there for what you have in your pocket.

Respect Starts With You

People treating you how you let them is only half the story. The other half is how you treat yourself when no one is watching. If you speak to yourself with patience, keep promises you make to yourself, and stop brushing off your own needs, people can't help but notice. That inner standard sets the tone. Eventually, the outside world follows the example you've already been living.

The Thing About Gossip

Gossip feels harmless at first. It's just talk, passing the time, sharing what "everyone already knows." But underneath, it says a lot more about the one spreading it than the person being talked about. When someone is quick to share other people's business, it often means they're avoiding their own. It's easier to point fingers outward than to look inward.

Gossip travels fast, but it rarely carries the whole truth. A story gets twisted, a detail gets exaggerated, and suddenly someone's reputation is being shaped by half-truths and guesses. Here's the part people don't like to admit: if someone gossips to you, they'll almost certainly gossip about you. That's the cycle. It's a habit. That's why it matters who you keep around. If the people closest to you thrive on tearing others down, eventually that energy will circle back. At the end of the day, gossip doesn't build anything. It doesn't solve problems or make life lighter. It just chips away at trust, piece by piece.

Strong people don't waste time spreading stories. They use that same energy to grow, to listen, and to handle their own business.

Gossip Lives at Home

Some families don't just gossip about neighbors or coworkers. They turn that same habit inward, aiming it at each other. What gets shared at the dinner table or whispered on the phone isn't about outsiders at all, but about a sibling's mistake or a cousin's struggle. In a house like that, no one feels safe, because anything done or said can become the story of the day.

This dynamic changes how people show up. Instead of being fully open, everyone learns to hold back. The cost is closeness. You can sit in the same room with family, but it feels like a performance, because honesty carries too much risk. So you hide parts of yourself, or even lie, just to avoid being the next subject. It also breeds competition. Gossip inside a family often works like a scorecard: who looks better, who slipped up, who has the upper hand, who has more money. It stops being about love and starts being about keeping an image. And when family ties are reduced to that, trust breaks quietly, long before anyone says it out loud.

The hardest truth is this: gossip in a family doesn't just bruise reputations. It bruises bonds. Outsiders can walk away, but inside the family, there is no leaving without consequence. That's why breaking the cycle matters. A family can't grow if every word is turned into fuel for the next conversation. Growth only begins when people realize that listening builds more than repeating ever could.

Silent Treatment

The silent treatment looks simple on the surface: no yelling, no name-calling, no fight. Just silence. But it cuts deeper than words. It's manipulation and punishment. It tells you that your voice, your presence, your existence isn't worth a reply. Toxic people use it to control. By refusing to speak, they force you to carry the tension, to second-guess what you did, to beg for answers. It shifts the weight onto you while they sit back with the power. That's why it feels so devastating. It's about making you feel small.

Over time, this treatment eats away at trust. You stop sharing honestly because you're afraid of being shut out. You walk on eggshells, avoiding conflict at all costs, just to escape the freeze-out. The damage isn't just in the moment. It lingers. Being ignored by someone close to you leaves marks long after the silence ends. You question your worth, your voice, your place. Real connection needs words, even hard ones. Silence used as a weapon doesn't protect relationships. It kills them.

Not Able to Care for Your Kids

Some realities are hard to say out loud, as they carry too much shame. One of those truths is what it feels like when you are not able to take care of your own children. Society tells us that being a parent should come naturally, that no matter what happens, you will always find a way. But the reality for many people is not that simple. Not being able to care for your kids can come from different circumstances: illness, poverty, addiction, trauma, or just being stretched too thin with no real support system. It does not matter which one; the result is the same. You are the parent, but you cannot do the job in the way you know your children deserve. That distance between what you want to give and what you can actually provide can eat away at you every single day.

The hardest part is the guilt. It shows up every minute of the day and night. You see it in the looks you think you catch on your child's face or in the way you measure yourself against other parents. You replay moments in your mind: missed school events, meals that were not healthy enough, times you were not emotionally present. The guilt piles up. People may tell you that you are doing your best, but when you look at your child, you know your effort is not meeting their needs. Then there is the judgment. Some of it is silent and imagined, but a lot of it is real. People assume that if you are not fully able to provide for your children, you must be lazy, careless, or unfit. They do not see the battles behind closed doors, the late nights trying to stretch a paycheck, the moments of breaking down in the bathroom so your kids will not hear you cry. They see failure when, in truth, what is happening is exhaustion and hardship.

What cuts deepest is the fear that your children will remember all of this. When they grow up, their memories of you will be about absence, struggle, or instability. You fear they will not see the love behind your efforts, only the gaps left by what you could not do. You wonder if they will resent you, or if they will grow up thinking they were not worth more. There is also anger at the world, at yourself. Anger that others have support systems you do not. That your own parents did not model better ways for you, and beneath that is grief: grief for the parent you wish you could have been, and grief for the childhood your kids might be missing out on.

Yet, even inside all of that, there is resilience. Parents who cannot take care of their kids in the way they want often spend every ounce of energy trying to fix things, even if progress is slow or invisible. They work extra shifts, reaching out for help even when it feels humiliating, and keep trying while carrying the burden of failure on their backs. The reality is this: not being able to care for your kids does not mean you do not love them. In fact, it often means the opposite, that the love you feel is so strong it is painful. The divide between your love and your life is what tears you apart.

And while society may not always understand, other parents who have been there do. They know that sometimes the strongest thing you can do is admit you are struggling rather than pretend you have it all together. It is not a neat story. It does not resolve with easy hope. But it is real. And sometimes, just telling the truth, without dressing it up or pretending it is lighter than it is, can be a form of care too.

Growing Up With a Narcissistic Mother

Not every mother is built for love. Growing up with a narcissistic mother means you learn early that her needs come before yours. Your existence must reflect her, to keep her satisfied. The rules in that type of home are unspoken but clear. You can be the trophy, the scapegoat, or the forgotten one, but you are never just a child.

The hardest part is the confusion. She can be warm and affectionate one moment, then cold and cutting the next. You never know which version of her you will get, so you stay on guard, constantly adjusting yourself even though nothing ever seems to be enough.

This shapes how you see yourself. You grow up questioning your feelings, doubting your memory. When you try to express hurt, it gets turned back on you.

"Too sensitive." "Too dramatic." "Ungrateful."

After a while, you stop speaking up. The outside world often does not see it. To neighbors, relatives, or friends, she might look charming, devoted, even selfless. You learn to smile in pictures, to keep the family secrets, and to play the role that makes her look good. People admire her, while you carry the private cost. The impact does not end when you leave home.

As an adult, you have a hard time keeping up with her demands. You struggle with boundaries, trust, and believing you deserve care that is unconditional.

You need endless reassurance from every partner of yours because deep down, you have a hard time believing they love you for yourself. And the worst part is, catching yourself hearing her voice in your head even when she is not there. The damage lingers. But recognizing it matters. Naming what happened helps break the hold.

A narcissistic mother does not define your worth, even if she made you believe that for years. The love you did not get is not proof you were unlovable; it is proof that she was not able to give it.

That difference is everything. The story does not end with her changing or apologizing. It ends when you begin to see the truth clearly and stop twisting yourself to fit her demands.

Then you can start building your own life.

Cost of Overloving

People don't always leave because things are broken. Sometimes they leave because they've been given more than they can carry. Too much attention, too much presence. What feels like love from one side can feel like pressure from the other. Over-loving often starts with good intentions. You want to protect the connection, make sure the person knows you care. But when every need is anticipated, and all the gaps are filled, it stops feeling like a partnership. One person is doing all the giving, and the other feels boxed in by it. The mistake isn't in loving. It is in not leaving room. People need space to be themselves inside a relationship. They need to feel they can choose when to step closer or step back. Without that freedom, even kindness begins to feel like control.

Losing someone this way is confusing because nothing "bad" seemed to happen. You gave effort, time, and attention, but the result was distance, not closeness. That is the lesson: more is not always better. Love that lasts doesn't smother. It makes room for breathing and silence, not demanding constant proof or presence. The challenge is to recognize when care tips over into pressure, and to pull back before it pushes someone away.

Cost of Cheating

Cheating is not a mark of cleverness. It is a sign of personal instability. People often cheat because they feel insecure, undervalued, or unhappy with their own lives. The motivations vary. Some cheat to feel desirable when they doubt their own worth. Others do it to inflate a fragile ego. Some believe that switching partners will fix their unhappiness. Different reasons, but the same pattern: running from what should be confronted.

What makes it destructive is not only the act itself but the refusal to face problems directly. The person chooses secrecy, so the issue remains unresolved, and now there is a breach of trust on top of it.

The consequences are wide. For the betrayed partner, the loss of trust is immediate and painful. For the person who cheats, the damage often leaves them worse off than before. Relationships rarely return to what they were once the foundation has been damaged. Cheating reveals weakness, avoids honesty, discipline, and rejects the discomfort of hard conversations. It is also a failure of judgment.

Intelligence involves recognizing problems and making decisions that improve life in the long run. But looking elsewhere does the opposite. It doesn't fix anything. It only spreads the damage further.

Two Sides of Love

Love can give us memories that last. A kind word, time spent together, or support when it mattered. These things stay. No one can take them away once they become part of you. Love can also cause damage. When trust breaks, and someone leaves because of that, the hurt does not disappear quickly. Sometimes it never fully heals. What once brought comfort now carries pain. This pain shows up in different ways. Some people avoid closeness. Others doubt themselves. For many, the hardest part is living with the reminders of what others did. Still, the hurt proves something important: love had meaning. It mattered enough to change you. That is why it leaves both memory and pain behind.

Love is not only joy but also hurt. It is both. It leaves marks you carry, whether they strengthen you or remind you of loss.

One Relationship at a Time

You can't be in a relationship and still make other people feel like they might matter in that way. Being with someone is a choice, and that choice means closing doors to other options. When you blur that line, you weaken the very thing you said yes to. Some people treat attention from others as harmless. They enjoy the ego boost or the feeling of being wanted. But when outsiders are left believing there's room for them, it isn't harmless. It disrespects the partner who expected your full loyalty.

What feels like nothing to you can look like betrayal to the one who trusted you. Respect demands consistency. If you want the freedom to explore other doors, don't enter a committed relationship in the first place. But if you do commit, then the expectation is clear: your attention belongs where you promised it would be. The truth is simple. A relationship is either a commitment or it isn't. You can't have it both ways. Trying to keep the benefits of commitment while also enjoying outside interests is unfair, dishonest, and damaging. It cheapens the bond you claimed to value.

If It's for Everyone, I Don't Want It

If anyone can have it, I don't want it. What's handed out to everyone means nothing. Value comes from being chosen, not from being available. Respect works the same way. If it's automatic, it isn't real. What matters is what's earned, not what's handed out for free.

I don't want leftovers, handouts, or what's been passed around.

If it doesn't stand apart, I'll walk away.

First Healthy Relationship After a Toxic One

Yes, toxic relationships are hard. But you know what else is hard? Your first healthy relationship after one.

The hardest part is how confusing it is to step into something safe when all you have known is chaos. You spend years walking on eggshells, explaining yourself over and over, or waiting for the next blow-up. When that becomes normal, it rewires how you think love works. So when you finally meet someone who treats you with respect, it does not always feel-good right away. It can feel strange, even unsafe. Unlearning those toxic habits takes work. You have to remind yourself that you do not need to defend every word, that not every silence means punishment, and that care does not always come with strings attached. It takes time to believe you do not have to live on alert anymore. You might push the healthy partner away to see if they stay or shrink back from affection because it feels overwhelming. You start to question their motives because your old life trained you not to trust anything.

So yes, healing inside a healthy relationship can feel lonelier than leaving a toxic one. At least in the toxic one, you knew the rules. In a healthy one, you are relearning from scratch. But staying with it matters. Over time, you start to notice that love can be consistent without being controlling. And slowly, you learn to stop fighting for what you deserve.

Learning to Walk Away

I keep telling myself I should have known better, that I should have seen the red flags sooner. It is easy to look back and blame yourself for not noticing what was right in front of you. But the truth is, everyone makes mistakes. We all believe what we want to believe. We all swallow lies when we want love to be real. What hurts the most is realizing that no matter how much you give, some people will never care the way you do. You can pour yourself into the relationship, and they will take every effort and sacrifice, acting like it was never enough. You end up exhausted, wondering what else you could possibly do, only to be let down every single time.

Walking away is not about giving up or not caring. It is recognizing that they will drain you and are never going to see your worth, only what they can take from you. So the hardest work is not leaving them, but making peace with yourself. You have to accept that you tried your best. You gave more than enough, and the failure was never yours to carry. It belongs to the one who refused to value you. Moving forward means realizing that they did not deserve you. The peace comes when you finally let go of the shame and stop replaying the mistakes. You start to see that your effort was real, even if their love never was.

A Father Who Favors His Son Over His Daughter

In a child's life, the deepest cut can come from a father's unfair choices. When a father consistently favors a son, the daughter learns early that love in her family comes with a ranking. As a child, there are no words for it, only a feeling. Each time the brother gets the attention, the praise, the approval that is denied to her, the message lands.

At first, the daughter tries harder. Be better, more agreeable, more helpful, more successful, so the father will notice too. Scan for the smallest signs that you matter. Yet it still feels like standing outside a circle you cannot step into. The brother belongs. The daughter is tolerated. That pattern cuts into a sense of worth. It is not just about fairness between siblings.

It shapes identity. If the person who was supposed to protect and treat you equally does not, the mind begins to argue that you are less and deserve less. Doubt sticks even when logic says otherwise. The heart keeps the score. The mind tries to erase.

Favoritism is not always loud. It can show up in who gets defended in an argument, who receives more freedom or more forgiveness, or in the simple habit of listening to the son's stories while cutting off the daughter mid-sentence. Small moments pile up until expectation changes: do not expect more.

Later, the impact shows up in places that do not look connected to a father at all. Trust gets shaky in relationships. Worth gets second-guessed at work and in friendships. Proving yourself becomes reflexive, even when no one asks. When equal respect finally arrives, belief comes slowly, since the foundation taught something different. The hardest part is that the father rarely sees it.

To him, it looks natural, even justified. He may say sons need more attention, or that daughters can handle less. The message to the daughter never changed: you do not count the way he does.

The truth to face is that his choice was never about her worth. His blindness is his failure. Real healing begins when the chase for what was never offered ends and a self is built outside his shadow. Being overlooked does not make a person invisible. Being treated as less does not make a person less.

The sharpest clarity arrives with this: approval is no longer required. A father who chose a son taught a hard lesson, but the daughter who lives through it carries what he never gave: the power to define her own value.

Difference Between Words and Actions

A lot of men know how to say the right things, to tell a woman she is beautiful, special, or loved. Words come easily, and for a moment, they can feel good. But anyone can memorize lines. What makes the difference is what follows. The right man backs up his words. He shows consistency and matches promises with action. That is what women remember in the long run. Not the phrases, but the way someone shows up when life is messy, stressful, or hard. The truth is simple: words can win attention, but actions build trust. And in the end, it is trust that keeps love alive.

Debt They Call Love Always Comes Due

Some people don't give. They trade.

Every gesture is a setup. Every "kindness" has a string. You figure it out when they remind you what you owe: the favor, the time, the loyalty. They keep score, and the balance is never in your favor. That isn't love. Real care doesn't keep receipts, demand payback, or bleed you dry just to feel whole. With them, it's not affection. It's a contract you never signed. And sooner or later, the bill comes due.

In the Name of Love, They Take

Family is supposed to be about love, support, and showing up for each other. But it doesn't always feel that way. At times, it feels like you're not a son, daughter, brother, or sister. You are just a tool. A favor machine. They always need something from you. Time, energy, effort. And they believe your money belongs to them, too.

You give, because that is what you have been taught family means. They don't see how much you need to work, the plans you cancel, the people you lose because of them, and all the stress you carry. They don't think twice about what it costs you.

Being used by family feels heavier than being used by strangers. You want to believe the people closest to you see you, respect you, and care about you. But when all they see is what you can do for them, it cuts deep.

At some point, you start to ask yourself: if family does not care what it costs you, is it still family?

In the end, I was me again, without him.

I woke up one morning and realized I had stopped wondering if he was happy, drinking, eating, or sleeping enough. The questions had starved me longer than they ever fed him. What remained was the only one that mattered: Was I alive now?

The answer was yes.

After that, days opened with new patterns, built on foundations that were mine alone. Plans no longer bent around another's demands but followed choices that finally belonged to me. His shallow world had stripped away my edges, leaving me unfamiliar to myself. Finding the way back hurt, but each step gave me air, carried me closer to who I was meant to be. My strength returned. Silence became a decision, not a cage anymore. The ache surfaced at times, but peace held stronger. Love that consumes identity is not love.

Confidence of the Foolish

Have you noticed how often the loudest voices in the room belong to those who understand the least? The ones who don't know much are usually the quickest to claim they know it all. They argue without hesitation, certain that their version of reality is the only one that matters. But that certainty does not come from wisdom. It comes from not seeing how complicated the world really is. When you take the time to learn, you find how messy things are. Every answer opens another question. Every idea has cracks.

People who know more usually carry some hesitation. They have seen enough angles to realize the truth is rarely simple. They speak with care, and that care is often mistaken for weakness. Meanwhile, the person who never looks beneath the surface walks around with their chest out. Their confidence is like a shield built from ignorance. They cannot imagine being wrong because they have never looked closely enough to see the possibility. Ironically, it is only through their stupidity that they manage to be so sure of themselves.

The real danger is how persuasive that kind of certainty can be. Many would rather follow someone who sounds confident than someone who speaks carefully. We mistake loudness for strength and hesitation for weakness. Wisdom is quieter. It does not rush to speak. It carries doubt, humility, and perspective. And maybe that makes it harder to notice, but far more trustworthy in the end.

Figure Moves

They pull the strings, and the figure moves. Every step is a response, not an act. The body bends, turns, and reacts, but nothing originates inside it. The motion isn't freedom. It is compliance. The scene looks like life from a distance, but up close it's mechanical. The one holding the strings decides what happens. The figure has no choice. It stands when lifted, collapses when dropped. The rhythm is not its own. It waits for direction, for a hand to make it count. The strings are not visible, but the control is. You can see it in the way the figure halts mid-motion, frozen until the next command comes. You can see it in the way its arms never rest in natural places, always pulled into shapes that fit someone else's need. The figure is not broken, but it is emptied. It has no voice. It cannot stop or walk away. The strings hold it in place, making it useful only as long as someone keeps pulling.

Last Meeting Theory

The last meeting theory says that any moment with someone could be the final one. You don't usually know when it happens. A normal talk, a quick laugh, an ordinary goodbye can later turn out to be the last time. Most people move through life assuming there will always be another chance, but sometimes there isn't. If you keep this in mind, it can change the way you act. You might hold back less, say what matters, or treat even small moments with more care.

This isn't about fear. It is about noticing what is already in front of you and not letting it slip away. Of course, no one can live with this thought every day. Life is full of noise and distraction. That doesn't make the idea useless. The point is not to follow it constantly but to remember it sometimes. It is more like a reminder, a way of seeing life differently now and then. That is when it becomes real, not as a rule, but as a sudden clarity that makes you pay attention.

Part of You That Still Waits

You tell yourself it's over, that you have moved on. You say the words out loud and maybe even half believe them. But deep inside, there's still a corner of you that waits, imagining the knock on the door, the message that says *I was wrong*, the voice that says *I never stopped loving you*. It's humiliating to admit, and you hate yourself for it. But that waiting part doesn't listen to logic or care how much time has passed or how many times they hurt you. It clings to possibilities like it's oxygen.

What makes it worse is how the world keeps feeding it. You see a story online about people finding their way back to each other. You hear a song that sounds like your own story, and suddenly that part of you believes again. It sits up, alert, ready, even though you know better. You can build a new life, make new memories, kiss someone else's mouth, and still, in the deepest crack of yourself, there's a ghost sitting on the edge of the bed, waiting. You don't talk about it, you don't let anyone see it. But it's there, alive and stubborn. Maybe one day it will die. Maybe one day you'll stop waiting.

But for now, you live with it, a small, bruised part of you forever leaning toward a door that will probably never open again.

Myth of Being Liked

It's wild how much energy people put into their reputation, like it's some priceless thing they need to keep spotless in case the world suddenly starts handing out trophies for being admired. They lose sleep worrying about how they look to folks who wouldn't even slow down if they saw them stranded on the side of the road. Reputation is a performance. It runs on gossip, on assumptions, on one-off comments taken out of context, and whatever gets posted online under just the right lighting. Never reflects on who they actually are. More often, it's just a version of them someone invented in their own head. Meanwhile, their character gets shoved to the back like it's the last item on a long to-do list. That's the part of them that shows up when nobody's offering compliments. It's how they treat people when nothing is on the line, what they do when no one is around to clap for it. It lives in the small moments when it would be easier to cut corners, look the other way, or act like they don't care. So if anyone is going to pour their effort into anything, let it be the part of them that's real. The part that stays after the spotlight moves on.

That's where peace lives. That's the only part of them that can't be faked.

Why Asking for Help Feels So Hard

People talk a lot about how important it is to *reach out* when you're struggling, like it's easy and all it takes is sending a message or making a call. In reality, asking for help is one of the hardest things a person can do. Not because we don't want help, but asking for it feels like admitting defeat and saying, "I can't handle this," and many of us were raised to believe we always should.

To ask for help, you have to face a few fears at the same time.

First, the fear of burdening someone.

Most people who struggle are not afraid of being alone. They're just afraid of being *too much*.

They don't want to become the friend who always has problems, the one others whisper about, or feel responsible for.

It's easier to stay silent than to risk becoming someone else's obligation.

Then there's pride.

People don't want to be seen as weak, even when they're falling apart. It's not that they don't want support.

They just wish someone would *notice without them having to ask*.

They want care, not pity. Understanding, not rescue.

But the hardest part is admitting to yourself that you need help in the first place.

That's the moment everything becomes real.

Once you say it out loud, you can't keep pretending things are fine. Sometimes staying silent feels safer because silence lets you stay in denial.

What does it take to finally reach out? Not courage. It takes trust.

You have to believe that the person you turn to won't judge you, won't panic, won't try to fix you like a broken appliance.

You have to believe they'll stay, even if they don't know what to say or don't fully understand.

Most people don't need perfect advice; they just need proof that someone cares enough to be there.

So when someone reaches out, even with a simple "hey," understand how heavy that message might be for them.

Treat it with care. Don't say, "Why didn't you tell me sooner?" Don't flood them with solutions. Just say "I'm here. I'm glad you told me."

Help doesn't always look like saving someone. Sometimes it's just sitting beside them long enough for them to remember they aren't alone.

Past Always Shows Up in the Middle of the Day

Your past trauma doesn't wait for permission to show up. It barges in while you're at the grocery store comparing prices on bread, trying to enjoy a movie, or in the middle of laughing with someone you trust. One second you're fine, the next you're slammed back into a moment you thought you left behind. You don't get to choose the trigger. It's just one second to the other; suddenly, you're not in the present anymore. Your body reacts before your mind catches up: your heart races, your chest tightens, and you feel unsafe even when nothing is happening right in front of you. From the outside, people say "that was years ago" or "you just need to move on." They have never carried a body that still thinks danger is coming. They don't know the humiliation of breaking down without warning. They have never lived with the exhaustion of pretending you're fine just to avoid scaring anyone, or worse, hearing them say "get over it." Living this way has a cost. It wears down trust, interrupts joy, and changes how you move through the world. And no matter how much you want it gone, it shows up on its own terms. But here's the truth: carrying it this long, still moving through the days when it felt impossible, that is strength no one can see. You know how to keep going in the middle of a storm that doesn't end. And maybe the outside world will never understand what it costs you, but you do. You feel the weight, you fight through it. And even if it shows up again tomorrow, you already have proof that you've survived it before, and you will again.

Heart Finally Agrees with the Mind

Sooner or later, the tug of war between your heart and your mind comes to an end. For so long, the heart keeps finding reasons to hold on, believing there is still something worth saving, while the mind has already called it for what it is. That back and forth eats you alive. One moment you are certain, the next you doubt yourself again. You try to move forward, but the heart drags you back into the mess, the memories, and the fragile hope that somehow it might change. Yet it is already over. You just don't want to admit it.

Then one morning, almost without noticing, you wake up and realize you don't want it back anymore. You see their name, and it doesn't sting the same way. You hear the old songs, and instead of breaking you, they just sound like noise. That is when you know: something inside has let go. It is like setting down a game you should have stopped playing a long time ago. The rules are never fair, but you kept showing up because your heart wasn't ready to walk away. That is the power in those words, when you can finally say them out loud to yourself:

My heart finally agrees with my mind. Game over.

It is the end of the pull, the fight, the end of living with one foot in the past and the other in the present. And in that ending, you discover a beginning you never thought you would earn, a clean slate, and a beautiful life that finally belongs to you.

Money Matters More Than the Person

In some families, love and connection get measured by numbers. Who earns the most, who brings in the checks, who pays the bills? Instead of being valued for who you are, you're judged by what you provide. When money takes that place, the person behind it starts to disappear. This dynamic makes relationships feel transactional. Time spent together comes with conditions. Help is offered but later counted. Even affection can feel like it has a price tag.

Over time, the message is clear: your worth isn't in your character or your heart, it's in your balance sheet. It also creates division. Siblings, parents, and even children can be pitted against each other in comparisons. Who has more, who has less, who is winning? Instead of family being the place where differences are accepted, it becomes another stage for competition. And competition leaves little room for safety. The deeper harm is that trust begins to erode. If money is always the headline, the person feels like a footnote. That environment makes people guarded. They learn to protect their private struggles instead of sharing them, because they know the first response won't be care, it will be judgment.

When money matters more than the person, a family may look strong on the outside, but it's fragile within. Real bonds don't come from wealth; they come from the assurance that who you are is enough. Families only stay whole when the person is valued before the numbers. Otherwise, they show themselves for what they are: leeches.

Letting Go Becomes the Only Way to Survive

There was a time when that person felt like your entire world. Every choice seemed shaped by their presence, and for a while, you believed you had found the one place where you could rest and feel safe. You told yourself that love was strong enough to heal any crack, that being with them would carry you through. But slowly, you saw what was really happening. What once felt like home became unbearable. The very person you thought would lift you up was breaking you down. Admitting the truth was painful, but survival demanded it. You had to decide between holding on and losing yourself or letting go and reclaiming your strength. Walking away was not a weakness. You could not keep carrying a relationship alone. Love is meant to be shared, not poured endlessly into someone who returns it with betrayal. Staying would have cost you the best parts of who you are. Leaving hurt, but it was the only path back to yourself.

Burden of What You Never Said

There are things you never said to anyone, not once, to no one. You thought it was safer to keep it inside. Maybe you were ashamed, didn't have the words, or you thought no one would believe you. So you carried it, letting it grow until that secret split you in half. That's what trauma does sometimes. It makes you a container for things you don't want but can't let go of. What nobody tells you is that silence isn't neutral. It's active. It keeps the wound open. Every day you don't speak it, it grows heavier, tangled, complicated. Until one day you realize you're not carrying a secret anymore, you're carrying a prison.

And the truth is, the moment you finally let some of it out, maybe to a friend, maybe to a stranger, or even just to yourself in writing, the weight shifts. It doesn't vanish, but it changes. You realize your voice has power, and you don't have to live buried under what happened. Saying it doesn't undo what happened. But it cracks open a space where you can be you again, a little bit. The hardest part is deciding to speak. But sometimes, if you do, you find out you were never as alone as you thought. The decision is yours.

The Internet Isn't the Problem

Social media does not ruin relationships. The apps do not send the messages. The likes do not flirt on their own. The problem starts when someone decides to act single while claiming they are not. There is a difference between using social media and using it like you are available. Posting selfies is fine. Sharing memes is harmless. But when someone starts replying to strangers like they are free, sending risky messages, entertaining late-night conversations, or fishing for constant attention, that is not "just the internet." That is disrespect. People love to blame the platform because it is easier than admitting the truth. Instagram did not make anyone cheat. Snapchat did not force anyone to hide messages. TikTok did not make anyone follow their ex again. Those choices came from the person holding the phone.

Being loyal is not about avoiding temptation. It is about ignoring it. If someone is truly committed, they shut down anything that threatens their relationship. They do not leave room for doubt or play both sides. They do not post like they are single while enjoying the benefits of being taken.

A healthy relationship can survive social media with no problem. What it cannot survive is someone who wants public attention more than private respect.

The internet is not the enemy.

Acting single while claiming you are not.

Hope is Work for Some

People talk about hope as if it were simple. They say things will get better, that you just need to try harder. Work more. Stay strong. To them, hope is natural, as though it comes without effort, the way breathing does. Maybe the words are meant kindly, but they slide past the reality of what it feels like to wake up every morning with the same heaviness pressing down on your chest. Carrying that load isn't a matter of choosing the right attitude. Hope isn't a switch you can flip. Sometimes it's barely there, or worse, it is gone completely. They don't understand that for some of you, hope is work. It's not given, it's something you fight to hold onto every single day.

War Is Over, But You're Still Bleeding

I once read a quote online:

Is it a weakness to seek peace when the war inside has no survivors?

In my book, the answer is no. It's not a weakness.

It's mercy, something most people won't understand until they need it themselves. When the war inside has already taken everything, when the damage is done and there's nothing left to fight for, choosing peace isn't surrender. It's refusing to keep destroying yourself just to prove how strong you are. People think survival means pushing through at all costs. But sometimes, real survival means stopping. Putting down the weight you've carried for too long.

Finally saying:

-I don't want to bleed just to feel alive anymore.

-I don't want to keep reliving what broke me.

Peace is not the easy way out. It's the hardest choice to live without burning everything down inside you first. And that choice?

That's a strength most people will never recognize.

Walls That Saved Her

Don't dismiss the walls she built. They're the reason she's still here. What looked like distance to others was protection to her. Those walls weren't built out of pride. It's just that she learned the cost of being too open too quickly. The walls are her way of making sure she doesn't pay that cost again. Respecting those walls is part of respecting her. You don't tear them down by force, and you don't shame her for having them. If trust comes, it comes because she decided to lower those walls at her own pace. In the end, her walls are not a weakness. They are proof she kept going, and proof she valued herself enough to protect her own life when no one else would.

Don't judge them. They were the only thing that kept her safe.

Time They Came Was the Time It Was

People think timing changes the story. They make lists in their heads of who should have shown up sooner, who should have arrived later, and who should have stayed away completely. I do not buy it. You meet people when you do, and that moment is all you get. There is no alternate version where it works better or hurts less. It happens, it shapes you, and it stays. And if you're looking for a cleaner version of life where you only meet the "right" people at the "right" time, you will be waiting forever. You do not get to edit the sequence or swap out the ones who broke you for some gentler option. You take them as they came, you deal with what they left behind, and you keep moving. That is it. No rewrites. No refunds. And if it broke something in you, then that break is yours now.

You decide what to build from it.

Silent Inside Wars

The battles inside us are the ones we rarely speak about. A person living with depression still shows up for work. A parent stretched thin tries to keep a family together while acting like nothing is wrong. A student carries pressure that feels unbearable but says nothing, afraid of being judged. These wars don't sound like gunfire, but they take pieces out of a life. Part of what makes them so hard is that they can't be seen. We notice wounds on the outside, but not the ones left by grief, loneliness, or memories that still hurt. Talking about struggle often feels unsafe. In a culture that rewards control, people hold their words in, and the fight grows stronger. Shame makes it worse. Many think they should handle more, or that their pain doesn't count compared to others. They blame themselves, and that only pushes them further into isolation. The truth is, most of us are carrying something. Knowing this should change how we move through the world: patience when someone feels distant, care when they are struggling. We can't end these wars for them, but we can make sure they don't have to face them completely alone.

Shape of Their Hate

Haters don't hate at random.

They target the things they reach for but cannot hold, the lives they dream of but will never step into. Throw their anger at the people who remind them of what they lack, and what they fear they will never become. Hate is often nothing more than longing in disguise, a bitter echo of desire turned sour. It is the shadow that follows those who dare to shine in a way others cannot.

Silence That Comes After Violence

People talk about violence in terms of the act itself: the breaking, bruising, the noise that follows, and the chaos that swallows everything. What stays, though, isn't always the act. It's the silence afterward, when no one checks on you. A family pretending nothing happened. Friends avoid your eyes because they don't know what to say. Violence doesn't just injure the body or the mind. It shifts your place in the world until you feel pushed into exile. The aftermath stays with you. You hesitate to tell the truth and doubt whether your pain is real, yet still question yourself why you didn't escape. Silence becomes another wound. It teaches you that your story feels unwanted, that speaking might be too heavy for others to carry. So you keep it inside, wearing a normal face, laughing at the right moment. But underneath, the weight presses harder than the violence itself. Healing starts when you decide it's enough and begin to speak the words aloud for the first time, or when someone sits close enough to show they can carry the truth with you. Until then, you live in a half-life, where what happened is always present but never spoken.

PS

If you've lived it, you know the brutality and the loneliness that come with it. And silence does not get the last word. When you finally decide to refuse carrying it alone, something shifts. It doesn't erase the past or fix everything. But it proves your story matters enough to be told.

First Step

If there is something you really want, it means you already have what it takes to make it happen. You might not see the full path or know where it begins, but if the thought lives in you, it is there for a reason. So take the first step, even if you feel nervous or unsure. The feeling of not being ready is normal. With each step, the view changes. What once felt impossible starts to break into pieces you can handle. The unknown shrinks as action turns it into experience. That is how you build a bridge between where you are and where you want to be. And one day, you look back and realize you are no longer asking if you can. You are already living what you once only lived in your mind.

People Leave a Different Kind of Dirt

In the past, when I ended up in the mud, I still felt like some part of me stayed clean. Even when life was hard, when I was broke or broken or just barely holding on, there was something in me that still felt honest. Still felt mine. I let in people who wore masks too well, and I can no longer tell what was real. They smiled like it meant something. Their words sounded right, practiced even. And I let myself believe they cared. For a while, I believed them. Until the truth showed itself, and by then, it was too late. I blamed myself. Maybe I was too trusting. And I only saw what I wanted.

But none of that changes what happened. It does not erase what they did in the shadows or in plain sight. The worst hurt doesn't always come from enemies. It comes from the ones you thought were safe. And when it's over, you're the one left doubting your own gut, your memory, your worth. What they left behind wasn't just disappointment. It was a stain that didn't come from struggle. It came from giving trust to those who never earned it, from lowering my guard for the wrong ones. That kind of dirt clings deeper than mud ever did.

And the cruelest part is this: they left me feeling dirtier than life itself ever could.

An Entire World Built on a Fragile Mirror

When someone close to you begins to chase worth through ego or status, the ground between you shifts; what once felt like a place for connection turns into performance. The person is still there, but what you see is a version crafted for display, not for trust. At first, it seems harmless, a boast tucked into conversation or a need to be noticed, but soon the search for validation takes over. Success is used as proof, relationships are valued for admiration, and even setbacks are reshaped to guard the image they want to keep. Your place beside them changes. You are expected to confirm rather than to know them. Approval becomes the price of closeness, and without it, they feel betrayed. Their balance rests on what you reflect, leaving you unseen even when you are near. In public, they appear polished; in private, the fragility is clear. What remains is a choice. You can keep supporting the mirror they rely on, or you can step back to preserve your own clarity. Neither path is easy. Staying costs authenticity, leaving feels like a loss. Yet the person you miss, the one who was once open, may already be hidden behind their need for validation.

Not For Everybody

A man only feels insecure about a woman when he knows deep down that she deserves better than what he can give. That insecurity does not come from nowhere. It comes from the awareness that she is operating on a higher level, carrying herself with standards, with value, and with strength that he cannot match. He senses it. He sees it. And instead of rising to meet her where she stands, he falls back into the comfort of what is familiar to him, the kind of life and relationships that do not demand growth or accountability. That is why sometimes you have to let a man go. Especially a man who was never truly on your level to begin with. Holding onto him only drags you down into what he is used to, and that is not where you belong. The truth is simple. Not every man is built to handle a woman of depth, confidence, and worth. And that is not your burden to carry. You are not for everybody. And the moment you stop apologizing for that, you stop settling for less than you deserve.

Inner Peace

Inner peace isn't about having no problems. It's about how you handle them when they come. Life will always bring stress and uncertainty, but you get to choose how you respond. You will face hardship, but you don't need to let it control your state of mind. If you can pause before reacting, that space helps you stay balanced. Pay attention to your triggers. Notice what emotions rise up. Don't push them away, but don't let them take over either. Boundaries also matter. Say no when you need to, and protect your energy from what drains you. Peace won't erase struggle, but it will stop struggle from overwhelming you. That balance lets you keep moving without losing yourself.

The Ghost You Become

When you ghost another soul, you vanish too. You tear a page from your own book, leave your own story half written. You step out of the light you were meant to stand in. Every silence you give away is a silence you keep. Each door you close without speaking is a door you lock from the inside. You think you slip past their memory, but it is your reflection that grows thinner, your presence that fades in your own life. To ghost someone is to haunt yourself. Your spirit knows. It remembers the words you did not say, the love you would not honor. It also remembers the truth you could not carry. And until you return to face them and have the courage to face yourself, you walk as half a shadow.

No Longer Just the Pain

People like to talk about pain as if it is the point. Doctors chart it, counselors circle it, and friends ask about it. But under the sharp edge, there is something stranger, harder to describe.

Pain is a signal. It tells you that you have been struck, cut, broken, or betrayed. Once the alarm bell has rung long enough, there comes the heavy, dragging space that follows.

What comes after is not relief. It's a pause when the noise dims, and you think you might be free. It is the place where you learn that you still exist even after the collapse.

You wake up and realize you must live with the hole that has been left.

The wound becomes part of you, and the body or the mind reshapes itself around what is missing. Some never reach that place. They stay locked in the noise, replaying it until it becomes their entire vocabulary.

Others make it past the surface and find something unexpected.

What they find is persistence. Then habits form. New ways of moving, speaking, and seeing yourself. You may not even notice at first. One day, you reach for a cup with your weaker hand, and it works. You walk into a room, and you are not the person who suffered, but simply yourself.

This is the space no one advertises. Books and speeches praise recovery, the moment when you rise again.

But they rarely talk about this long middle ground where you are not triumphant and not destroyed. You are simply present. Taking the next step. It can feel disappointing.

You expect clarity or meaning to arrive as a prize for surviving. Instead, you get bills, laundry, conversations that drift, and socks left in the washing machine.

It means you have crossed into a territory where pain no longer dictates every line of your story.

You are building a life on ground that once felt unlivable. It is not a miracle or sudden light or redemption. It is the slow accumulation of days in which you keep showing up.

Proof that even when pain has screamed itself hoarse, life goes on in your hands.

Where the Light Forgot to Land

Some people grow up waiting for something that doesn't come. No miracle, no second chance.

There are houses where no one talks about what matters. Rooms where silence replaces honesty and gossip about others becomes normal. What's earned matters more than who you are, and being useful replaces being known.

And if you're different, the damage this left in you is sometimes irreversible. Then you grow up, you go to work, doing what you're supposed to. Yet still, something important is missing. You don't see it when you're young.

You believe this is how things are. And love is something you prove, not something you feel.

Safety means not getting in trouble and hiding what hurts. You learn to be invisible in all the ways that count, say exactly what others want to hear, and expect nothing more than the bare minimum.

Later, when you see how different some other people's lives are, it hits you.

They have something you didn't know was possible: warmth, openness, consistency. Not just moments of it, whole days, whole years. And it hits you again. You grew up in a place where the light never came.

That realization can break you slowly. You start to wonder what parts of yourself never had a chance to develop and how much of your personality is just adaptation, and maybe your strength is just a response to neglect.

You ask yourself if people would still like you if you weren't always trying so hard.

There's no redemption arc here. Not yet. Maybe not ever. There's no big shift or sudden clarity. Just this fact: it happened. You lived through something you didn't deserve. It shaped you. You carry it. And maybe the light won't come later either.

And the best you can do is stop pretending you don't notice the cold.

Maybe it's about naming the absence. Saying it out loud. Not for pity. Just for truth. There are stories that never get fixed and people who never get back what they lost.

That doesn't make them weak. It makes them real. And that's what matters. Not becoming someone else or fixing everything.

Just being able to say: this is where the light forgot to land, and I'm still here.

Edge of Letting Go

Loving someone deeply doesn't guarantee they're right for you. Affection alone doesn't mean they rise to your needs, or that their presence lifts you higher. What feels powerful in your heart doesn't always translate into what's healthy for your life. When that truth is clear, leaving still cuts deep. The mind may recognize their shortcomings, but the heart remembers the moments that made you stay. Attachment lingers; pain outweighs joy, while hope collides with reality again and again. You know they fall short, yet part of you still clings to the comfort of what once was, as you stand at the edge of letting go.

Grief Nobody Brings Flowers For

When someone dies, people show up with flowers, casseroles, and cards. They gather around you, acknowledging your grief. Yet when a relationship ends, no one comes knocking with lilies. No one says, I'm sorry for your loss.

Still, it is a loss. It's the death of a future you built in your head. It's the end of rituals, anniversaries, and inside jokes. You don't get a funeral to mark it. Or sympathy that lasts longer than a day or two. People expect you to get over it because nobody died. But something did die. It just doesn't have a grave. So you grieve alone, carrying it by yourself, and move through all the seven stages. Shock, denial, anger, bargaining, depression, testing, acceptance. And that makes it lonelier than death sometimes.

PS

Elisabeth Kübler-Ross first described five stages of grief. Later writers and clinicians expanded the model to seven, adding shock at the beginning and testing before acceptance. Psychologists call this disenfranchised grief: the very real grief of a breakup or relationship loss that often goes unrecognized, even though it is as valid as mourning a death. But it's important to remember that not everyone moves through each stage, or in this exact order.

For the ones too blind to see the truth

The heartbreaking truth is that constantly showing and proving you are better, trying to make other people see what they lost, never truly validates you. Putting yourself out and flashing, look who I am, only traps you in a constant performance, waiting for other people to clap and appreciate you, because the one who is with you, or was with you, did not really do that. And that performance never ends. You run yourself in circles, exhausted, still questioning if it is enough. The reality, even if it sounds very bad, is that when you are irreplaceable to them, they never even think about leaving you. And if they do, it means they are missing something they cannot get from you, or maybe they are just not happy with one person and need constant excitement from others.

Well, that is on them, not on you. Validation is different. It is not about applause or competition. When it is real, they do not need you to measure up or to win. They see you, hear you, and affirm your worth just as you are. But if someone does not love you wholeheartedly, you end up betrayed, or worse, carrying the humiliation of their actions, while at the same time, you are not even aware that a complete stranger, even a supposed enemy, is defending you without really knowing you. That is the lesson you need to learn. Every person, just like you, has two sides. One in public and one behind closed doors. And if your partner betrayed you, not once, but several times, then it is time to close that chapter, because it will keep happening again. Maybe the next time you are not going to know about it, because they also learned their lesson, how to hide their trace better than before. You need to respect yourself more. Because if you don't, you hand them the power to write your worth for you again.

Don't Treat Yourself Like a Broken Phone

There's a habit many of us fall into without realizing it: treating ourselves like a project in constant need of repairs. A passing remark, a raised eyebrow, a dismissive glance, and suddenly you're tightening screws that were never loose, sanding down edges that gave you your shape.

It begins quietly. You tell a joke, no one laughs, and the thought creeps in: *Maybe I should talk less.*

You share your excitement about something you love, someone shrugs, and you wonder if you should hold back next time. Before long, you're scanning yourself like faulty code, too loud, too emotional, too opinionated, too much. You start updating yourself as if you're outdated software that has to keep pace with the versions others demand.

The people who set this in motion rarely notice. They're not applauding when you hold back, and they're not handing out medals when you swallow your words. They never see the invisible effort, the energy it drains, the way it makes you smaller.

And here's the truth: they don't deserve it. Not your revisions, not your edits, not the hours you spend reshaping yourself into something "more acceptable." If someone only connects with the watered-down version, they're not connecting with you at all. They're agreeing with a stranger you built in their image. That isn't love, and it isn't friendship. It's a mirage.

The hardest realization is how many times you've thought, *If I just adjust this one last thing, maybe they'll finally treat me the way I need.*

But every change only shifts the target. You're never finished. By the time you see it, you're running on fumes, patched together with self-doubt, while the very people you're striving for remain unaware. You're not broken. You don't need fixing. You don't need to hand anyone the blueprint of yourself to prove your worth.

The better question isn't *What's wrong with me? Why am I pouring so much into those who don't even see me?* You're not a repair shop, a prototype, or a product awaiting approval.

You're allowed to exist as you are, without twisting into shapes that only fit someone else's narrow frame. If a person makes you feel like too much, that's not your cue to shrink. If they make you feel like not enough, that's not your signal to push harder. It's proof they were never your people.

So stop handing your light to those who only notice the scratches. If they can't see your shine without edits, they don't deserve a seat at your table.

The Day My Eyes Took Over

I used to think I knew what you looked like, but that wasn't true. I hadn't really been seeing you with my eyes. I was filling in the blanks with what I wanted you to be. The heart does that. It edits the picture. Then one day, I finally looked at you without all that interference. Just you, in plain sight. And it was jarring. You weren't beautiful. Not even close. The strange part is you hadn't changed. My vision had. The way I used to see you was all imagination, all hope. It made something out of nothing. And once that collapsed, there was no going back.

That was the moment I realized: the heart lies, and the eyes don't.

PS

And that lesson isn't only about you. It's about everything. How many times do we let ourselves believe in an illusion just because it's easier, softer, more comfortable than the truth? We edit reality because it hurts less. But when the truth finally shows up, it gives us something far stronger than comfort: clarity. That is what sets you free and keeps you from wasting years chasing a mirage. The day my eyes took over was the day I stopped letting illusions tell me who someone was, what I deserved, or what my life should look like. The eyes don't lie. They strip away the disguise, show you what's real.

And when you finally choose to see without the filters, you get the chance to live without lies.

Victim Play That Never Ends

Toxic people love to cling to that position as if it is the only one they know. When conflict shows up, they bend the story until they appear hurt or unfairly treated. This is not random. It is a skill practiced for years. While most children grow up learning honesty through trial and error, these people were learning to plant doubt and pull sympathy when they were at fault. In time, it stopped feeling like a trick. It became a habit they used without effort. That is why deception feels easy for them. They do not lose their focus or look away. Their words come out smooth, as if nothing is wrong. Because they have done it for so long, others cannot always tell the difference between false pain and the real thing.

By placing themselves as the injured one, they push everyone else into positions they never asked for: the helper, the comforter, the apologizer, or even the scapegoat. People around them start doubting themselves, asking if they were too harsh or too demanding. That pause is what the manipulator waits for. Doubt is their sharpest tool. The painful part is that while others are lost in self-questioning, the manipulator has already taken what they wanted. They have escaped blame, drawn attention, and secured control. It is not only about telling lies. It is about reshaping the setting so they remain in charge. Once the cycle is seen, it no longer convinces. The stories that sounded real reveal themselves as habits repeated over the years. What seemed like hurt shows itself as a tactic refined with time.

She Wants to Leave, but is So Afraid

The thought of leaving shows up more often than she admits. It comes when the house is quiet, when bruises ache that no one else can see. She pictures herself walking out, bag in hand, finally free. Then the fear rushes in. What if he finds her? What if no one believes? What if she can't make it on her own? So many what-ifs. The dream of leaving is strong, but the fear is stronger. Fear is how he keeps her there. Not just fear of what he'll do if she goes, but also of what life might look like without him. He has chipped away at her confidence for so long that she questions whether she's even capable of starting over. He's made her believe she is weak, dependent, broken.

And so she stays, even though every part of her wants out. To convince herself, she repeats that it's safer this way. Keeping the peace feels easier than risking the storm. Maybe tomorrow will be different. Maybe he will change. Deep down, she knows those are lies, but they soften the weight of fear enough to get through another day. What outsiders don't see is that leaving isn't a simple choice. It's not just packing a bag and stepping out the door. To her, it's like stepping into the unknown with no safety net. Years of abuse have taught her to expect punishment for every act of defiance, so the thought of escape feels like an inviting danger. Fear binds her to the very place that's breaking her. Until the moment comes when the need for freedom outweighs the terror, she will keep imagining the door, standing on the other side of it, too afraid to open.

Responsibility in Relationships

In relationships, responsibility is more than just taking care of practical tasks. It includes emotional accountability, honesty, and the willingness to face conflicts directly. When responsibility is avoided, the connection begins to weaken. Instead of solving problems together, you get caught in a cycle of avoidance and blame. One common pattern is the refusal to admit mistakes. If an argument escalates, you insist that everything was caused by the other person. You may replay the situation in a way that removes your role entirely. Over time, this leaves the other person feeling unheard and unfairly judged, building resentment as they carry the weight for both of you. Blame shifting can also look like deflection. When bills are late, you insist that the other person should have remembered. When plans fall through, you say it was their fault. In conflicts about emotional needs, you dismiss concerns as unreasonable. This blocks real communication and leaves the other person defending themselves while you avoid engaging honestly. The long-term impact is damaging. If you refuse to acknowledge your role, the other person learns that honesty will not be met with fairness. Even if the relationship continues, intimacy fades, replaced by frustration and exhaustion. This same pattern shows up in families. A parent might place blame on a child for tension in the home, or siblings may deflect mistakes by pointing to each other's flaws. These patterns create cycles of conflict where no one feels safe to be vulnerable. The path forward begins with self-awareness. Taking responsibility does not mean taking all the blame. It means recognizing the part you play and admitting when you fall short. When both people are willing to own mistakes and learn from them, relationships grow stronger through the very challenges that once threatened them.

Light Within

When you carry light inside, you are never truly lost. It may not be seen with the eyes, but it guides your heart and points the way forward. No matter how far you travel or how uncertain the path becomes, inner light gives you clarity to keep moving. It cuts through confusion and helps you take the next step when everything around you feels unclear.

Home is not always a physical place. It can be the comfort of belonging, sometimes the peace of being understood, or the feeling of safety when you are with the right people. Wherever home is found, the light within acts as a reminder that you still belong there. In struggle or doubt, that glow inside whispers that the way back is never gone.

This light cannot be taken away by hardship or distance. It remains, no matter how far you feel you have wandered. And when you choose to trust it, you realize something important: the journey may bend and change, but it will not break you. That light in your heart is enough to hold you, every time, until you arrive again at the place you call home.

Price of Overthinking

You know how overthinking disguises itself as preparation. You convince yourself that if you replay every scenario, word, or possible outcome, you'll be ready. You imagine that rehearsing worst-case scenarios will protect you, like stacking sandbags against a flood. But the truth is, pain still arrives when it wants to, no matter how many nights you stay awake rehearsing it. That habit trades today's peace for tomorrow's fear. It makes your body restless, your mind loud, and your relationships tense. You think you're controlling the future, but really you're surrendering the present. The minutes you lose to mental loops don't return. They just leave you drained when the real challenges show up.

And people will say, "Just stop overthinking." You've heard that advice in quick slogans and surface-level reminders. But slowing a thought spiral is rarely simple. When the habit is strong, stepping away feels dangerous, as if you're ignoring something important. Letting go of a cycle can feel like standing unarmed in front of uncertainty. It's uncomfortable, sometimes unbearable. Still, there's no way around it. It doesn't stop betrayal from hurting, failure from stinging, or grief from hollowing you out. The hurt comes whether you anticipate it or not. That cycle makes you hurt twice: once in advance, in your imagination, and again when reality unfolds. Recognizing this won't dissolve the habit overnight. But noticing the cost, seeing the way it steals your hours and weakens your resilience, can help you pause. Even if it is imperfect, that pause is proof you can step outside the loop, and that is where peace begins.

The real meaning of the upgrade in a relationship

People often think of an "upgrade" after a relationship as someone who looks better, dresses sharper, or seems more impressive on the surface. But that's not what it really is. Looks can fade quickly. A true upgrade is about how you are treated. It is someone who listens when you talk instead of brushing you off and notices the small details about you. A person who values your time, your feelings, and your presence, not just what you give them.

That is the difference between feeling invisible and feeling seen. Finally being able to be yourself. Feeling respected, appreciated, and secure. In your last relationship, you may have settled for less, thinking that was normal or all you deserved. That is why the real upgrade is not about the outside package but the inside reality. It is someone who does not just say you matter but shows it in how they treat you day after day.

Bridge Between Thought and Action

Starting anything requires a crossing.

There is always a space between the spark of an idea and the moment it becomes real. That space can feel wide, like a river you cannot leap in a single bound. What carries you across is the bridge. It might be one small step, a note scribbled down, a call made, or a single word written on a page. That bridge does not have to be grand; it only has to exist. Without it, plans remain locked inside the mind. Dreams stay folded away, living in imagination but never in the world. But with it, with even the smallest bridge, what once lived only in thought takes its first step into action.

A Real Woman Knows

They said;

"A real woman knows how to keep a man."

I don't agree with that theory.

A real woman knows she's not a full-time therapist for insecure men.

If someone needs constant praise, proof, or supervision to stay loyal, that's not a partner, that's unpaid emotional labor.

Adults don't get "kept."

They step up or step out.

Living Life on Your Own Terms

People will always have opinions about how you should live, where to work, how to dress, and who to be with. They even give opinions on who you should love. At first, it seems easier to agree. You get less judgment and keep the peace. But over time, you start to feel like you are watching someone else live your days. Trying to please everyone drains your energy. It never ends. Once you satisfy one person, another steps in with a new demand. You also notice something else. The people you are trying to impress are not always happier for it. They move on with their lives, while you are left with choices that were never yours. Living for yourself does not mean ignoring others. It means making your own decisions first. Listen to advice.

Think about it. Then choose what actually feels right. You know your goals better than anyone. You also know what makes you miserable. That is reason enough to set a boundary. Some people might not like it when you finally speak up. They may call you selfish. Let them talk. There is nothing selfish about taking control of your own life. When you choose your path, you become more honest and more present. You also become easier to trust. People can sense when you are being real.

Life is short. If you spend it chasing approval, you will never feel satisfied. If you spend it building something that matters to you, even the struggle feels worthwhile. In the end, you are the one who has to live with your choices, so they should be yours.

If You Interfere in My Life, I Will Interfere in Yours

Some people think they can push into your life, spread lies, create drama, and then stand back like they did nothing. They act bold because they believe you are brainless and will stay silent because you're scared. What they fail to understand is that silence is not fear. It is a restraint.

The rule is simple: if you cross into my life with bad intentions, do not be shocked when I step into yours. I do not go looking for problems, but I will never run from them. So let it be known; I know who you are, even when others don't. You can play games, whisper behind my back, pretend you know more than you do. You may think you are clever. But tricks do not work on someone who already sees through you. You should be more worried about my silence than my words. It means I have already made a decision.

And that alone should be enough for you to stay in your lane.

Not Everything Can Be Fixed With "Sorry"

People love to think that an apology solves everything. They'll hurt you, lie to you, betray your trust, and then toss out a quick *"I'm sorry"* like it's a magic reset button. Maybe it works on some people. But not on the ones who truly felt the damage.

It's simple; there are wounds that go deeper than words can reach. Some actions don't break the skin; they break the spirit. Once someone has shown you that they are capable of cutting you that deeply, their apology doesn't erase the memory or remove the moment you realized they didn't value you the way you valued them.

An apology may show regret, but it doesn't guarantee change. Words are easy. Effort is proof. So, no "sorry" doesn't always fix it. Sometimes, the most respectful response you can give is silence, and the real closure is moving on without reopening the door. Not every wound needs a bandage. Some just need distance.

You Can't Pour Into a Broken Bucket

Your praise, your touch, your constant reassurance never landed inside him.

You gave him oceans of validation every single day, but his bucket had a hole in the bottom. No matter how much you poured in, it drained out almost instantly. The belief that he was enough never stayed.

He did not believe it about himself, so he could not hold it when you offered it.

So he kept chasing cheaper and faster hits from strangers. Random smiles, flirty texts, new numbers in his phone. Fresh proof he mattered. For thirty brief seconds, attention from someone new gave him what your years of consistency never could. Worthy.

It was never about you failing. Just his inability to receive anything real.

You could have told him he was the most handsome man alive every minutes and touched him with complete devotion, and that hole would still be there, leaking.

That is the cruel part. People who love with depth often lose to people who love with the least effort, because the easy ones feed the addict the quick fix he is wired to chase.

You did not fail at loving him. He failed at letting himself be loved.

No amount of your daily effort could repair a belief he refused to confront. That is why he did what he did. Not because you fell short, but because he never learned how to feel full.

That is also why it felt exhausting. You were not dating only him. You were carrying his insecurity and every woman he used to calm it.

Real love does not need a scoreboard built from other people's desire.

What you had was meaningful, but his addiction to validation poisoned it. You did not lose a great love. You stepped out of a dynamic where your peace was always the cost of his ego.

That is why the air feels easier now. You are no longer holding his emptiness.

I Wasn't Saved. I Saved Myself

There are things I have lived through that most people will never understand. If I tried to explain it, I would not even know where to begin. The beatings. The fear. The way I trained myself to stay silent because speaking only brought more pain. I was hurt in ways no one should ever experience. I bled while someone stood there and watched. I cried while they laughed.

There were days I truly did not know if I would make it. Bruises made it hard to walk. Fear made it hard to lift my head or speak. Survival was not living. It was performing.

What cut deeper than the violence was knowing it came from someone I once trusted. My pain was their entertainment. But one day, something inside me refused to stay silent. I made a decision. I would not take it anymore. I planned my escape. I did not walk out confident. I walked out exhausted. But I walked out. People think healing means forgetting. It does not. I will remember for the rest of my life. The memory lives in my body. But now I am free. The tears are gone. The fear is gone. What remains is anger turned into strength.

Justice may not come in this world, but God saw everything. One day he will answer for what he did. I am not the woman I was back then. I am stronger and capable of love again. I have peace now. A home. A life built on faith, not fear. Nobody rescued me. I rescued myself.

I carry scars, but I am not anyone's victim. I am proof that pain can be survived. And once you claim your freedom, you never give it back.

Room That Can't Save You

So many people lie to themselves about healing after they are cheated on. They think if they change the furniture, repaint the walls, or clean up the mess, the room turns into something new. It doesn't. A place that broke you does not stop breaking you just because it looks different.

You can scrub the history out of the corners, but the memory that your partner touched someone else, betrayed your trust, stays in the air.

You still walk the same floor where you learned to shrink yourself. You still sit in the same space where you stopped speaking your mind. Your body recognizes what your pride tries to forget. That room trained you to survive by making yourself smaller. It will not teach you anything else.

People stay because familiarity feels easier than change. They convince themselves they can rebuild in the same environment that damaged them. They call it forgiveness or maturity. It is usually fear. Healing does not come from repainting the past.

Healing starts when you leave the place that taught you to accept less than you deserved.

You cannot grow in a space that benefits from your weakness or heal in a place that learned to function by watching you fall apart. Leaving is not quitting. It is just the first honest thing you do for yourself.

Some places are not meant to be fixed. They are meant to be walked out of.

www.ingramcontent.com/pod-product-compliance
Lightning Source LLC
Chambersburg PA
CBHW071727120626
46550CB00002B/413